lonely planet

Fast Talk

Spanish

Guaranteed to get you talking

Contents

⩦ Special Features

Before You Go

Although English is relatively widely spoken in Spain, just a few phrases go a long way in making friends, inviting service with a smile, and ensuring a rich and rewarding travel experience – you could order delicious tapas in a bar packed with locals, find a hidden art gallery or grab a great shopping bargain from a hot new designer.

PRONUNCIATION TIPS

The sounds of Spanish can almost all be found in English, and if you read our coloured pronunciation guides as if they were English you'll be understood. The stressed syllables are indicated with italics.

★ The few sounds that do differ from English include the strong, rolled r, and the harsh, throaty kh (as in the Scottish *loch*).

★ Also note that the Spanish v is soft, pronounced almost like a 'b' (with the lips pressed together), and that ly is pronounced as the 'li' in 'million'.

★ You may have heard that Spanish has a 'lisping' th sound. In fact, when you hear the Spanish say *gracias* gra·thyas, they are are no more lisping than when you say 'thank you' in English.

MUST-KNOW GRAMMAR

The structure of Spanish holds no major surprises for English speakers since the two languages are quite closely related.

★ Spanish has a formal and informal word for 'you' (*Usted* oo·*ste* and *tú* too respectively). When talking to someone familiar or younger than you, use the informal *tu* form.

Phrases in this book use the form that is appropriate to the situation. Where both forms can be used, they are indicated by **pol** and **inf** respectively.

★ Spanish also distinguishes between masculine and feminine forms of words, eg *bello/bella* be·lyo/be·lya (beautiful), indicated in this book by **m** and **f**.

★ Verbs have a different ending for each person, like the English 'I do' vs 'he/she do**es**'. Travellers don't need to worry too much about this though – if you use the dictionary form of a verb in all contexts, you'll still be understood.

SOUNDS FAMILIAR?

Numerous Spanish words are already part of the English vocabulary – you're sure to recognise *armada, aficionado, embargo, fiesta, machismo, patio, plaza, salsa* ...

Fast Talk Spanish

Don't worry if you've never learnt Spanish (*español* es·pa·nyol), or Castilian (*castellano* kas·te·lya·no) as it's also called in Spain, before – it's all about confidence. You don't need to memorise endless grammatical details or long lists of vocabulary – you just need to start speaking. You have nothing to lose and everything to gain when the locals hear you making an effort. And remember that body language and a sense of humour have a role to play in every culture.

"you just need to start speaking"

Even if you use the very basics, such as greetings and civilities, your travel experience will be the better for it. Once you start, you'll be amazed how many prompts you'll get to help you build on those first words. You'll hear people speaking, pick up sounds and expressions from the locals, catch a word or two that you know from TV already, see something on a billboard – all these things help to build your understanding.

5. Phrases to Learn Before You Go

1. What time does it open/close?
¿A qué hora abren/cierran? a ke o·ra ab·ren/thye·ran

The Spanish tend to observe the siesta (midday break), so opening times may surprise you.

2. Are these complimentary?
¿Son gratis? son gra·tees

Tapas (bar snacks) are available pretty much around the clock at Spanish bars. You'll find they're free in some places.

3. When is admission free?
¿Cuándo es la entrada gratuita?
kwan·do es la en·tra·da gra·twee·ta

Many museums and galleries in Spain have admission-free times, so check before buying tickets.

4. Where can we go (salsa) dancing?
¿Dónde podemos ir a bailar (salsa)?
don·de po·de·mos eer a bai·lar (sal·sa)

Flamenco may be the authentic viewing experience in Spain, but to actively enjoy the music you'll want to do some dancing.

5. How do you say this in (Catalan/Galician/Basque)?
¿Cómo se dice ésto en (catalán/gallego/euskera)?
ko·mo se dee·the es·to en (ka·ta·lan/ga·lye·go/e·oos·ke·ra)

Spain has four official languages, and people in these regions will appreciate it if you try to use their local language.

10. Phrases to Sound Like a Local

What's up?	**¿Qué pasa?**	ke *pa*·sa
Great!	**¡Genial!**	khe·*nyal*
How cool!	**¡Qué guay!**	ke gwai
That's fantastic!	**¡Estupendo!**	es·too·*pen*·do
Really?	**¿En serio?**	en *se*·ryo
You don't say!	**¡No me digas!**	no me *dee*·gas
Sure.	**Seguro.**	se·*goo*·ro
OK.	**Vale.**	*va*·le
Of course!	**¡Por supuesto!**	por soo·*pwes*·to
Whatever.	**Lo que sea.**	lo ke *se*·a

10. Phrases to Start a Sentence

When's (the last flight)?	¿Cuándo sale (el último vuelo)? *kwan·do sa·le (el ool·tee·mo vwe·lo)*
Where's (the station)?	¿Dónde está (la estación)? *don·de es·ta (la es·ta·thyon)*
Where can I (pay)?	¿Dónde puedo (pagar)? *don·de pwe·do (pa·gar)*
How much is (the room)?	¿Cuánto cuesta (la habitación)? *kwan·to kwes·ta (la·bee·ta·thyon)*
Do you have (a map)?	¿Tiene (un mapa)? *tye·ne (oon ma·pa)*
Is there (a toilet)?	¿Hay (servicios)? *ai (ser·vee·thyos)*
I'd like (a coffee).	Quisiera (un café). *kee·sye·ra (oon ka·fe)*
Can I (enter)?	¿Se puede (entrar)? *se pwe·de (en·trar)*
Can you please (help me)?	¿Puede (ayudarme), por favor? *pwe·de (a·yoo·dar·me) por fa·vor*
Do I have to (book)?	¿Necesito (reservar)? *ne·the·see·to (re·ser·var)*

Chatting & Basics

≡ Fast Phrases

Hello./Goodbye.	Hola./Adiós. *o·*la/*a·dyos*
Please./Thank you.	Por favor./Gracias. por fa·*vor*/*gra·*thyas
Do you speak English?	¿Habla inglés? pol *ab·*la een·*gles* ¿Hablas inglés? inf *ab·*las een·*gles*

Essentials

Yes./No.	Sí./No. see/no
Please.	Por favor. por fa·*vor*
Thank you (very much).	(Muchas) Gracias. (*moo·*chas) *gra·*thyas
You're welcome.	De nada. de *na·*da
Excuse me.	Perdón./Discúlpeme. per·*don*/dees·*kool·*pe·me
Sorry.	Lo siento. lo *syen·*to

Fast Talk **Addressing People**

Señor se·*nyor* (Mr), *Señora* se·*nyo*·ra (Ms/ Mrs) and *Señorita* se·nyo·*ree*·ta (Miss) tend to be used in everyday speech. *Doña* do·nya, although rare, is used as a mark of respect towards older women, while *Don* don is sometimes used to address men. You may hear friends calling each other *tío* m *tee*·o or *tía* f *tee*·a (literally 'uncle' and 'aunt'), and these words are also used when talking about others.

Language Difficulties

Do you speak English?	¿Habla inglés? pol *ab*·la een·*gles* ¿Hablas inglés? inf *ab*·las een·*gles*
Does anyone speak English?	¿Hay alguien que hable inglés? ai al·*gyen* ke *ab*·le een·*gles*
Do you understand (me)?	¿(Me) entiende? pol (me) en·*tyen*·de ¿(Me) entiendes? inf (me) en·*tyen*·des
I don't understand.	No entiendo. no en·*tyen*·do
I speak a little Spanish.	Hablo un poco de español. *ab*·lo oon *po*·ko de es·pa·*nyol*
What does ... mean?	¿Qué significa ...? ke seeg·nee·*fee*·ka ...
How do you pronounce this?	¿Cómo se pronuncia esto? *ko*·mo se pro·*noon*·thya *es*·to
How do you write ...?	¿Cómo se escribe ...? *ko*·mo se es·*kree*·be ...

Could you please repeat that?	¿Puede repetirlo, por favor? *pwe*·de re·pe·*teer*·lo por fa·*vor*
Could you please write it down?	¿Puede escribirlo, por favor? *pwe*·de es·kree·*beer*·lo por fa·*vor*
Could you please speak more slowly?	¿Puede hablar más despacio, por favor? *pwe*·de ab·*lar* mas des·*pa*·thyo por fa·*vor*
✂ Slowly, please!	Más despacio, por favor. mas des·*pa*·thyo por fa·*vor*

Greetings

Hello./Hi.	Hola. o·la
Good morning.	Buenos días. *bwe*·nos *dee*·as
Good afternoon.	Buenas tardes. *bwe*·nas *tar*·des
Good evening/night.	Buenas noches. *bwe*·nas *no*·ches
See you later.	Hasta luego. *as*·ta *lwe*·go
Goodbye./Bye.	Adiós. a·*dyos*
How are you?	¿Qué tal? ke tal
Fine, thanks. And you?	Bien, gracias. ¿Y Usted/tú? pol/inf byen *gra*·thyas ee oos·*te*/too

11

Titles

Mr	Señor se·*nyor*
Ms/Mrs	Señora se·*nyo*·ra
Miss	Señorita se·nyo·*ree*·ta

Introductions

What's your name?	¿Cómo se llama Usted? **pol** *ko*·mo se *lya*·ma oos·*te* ¿Cómo te llamas? **inf** *ko*·mo te *lya*·mas
My name is ...	Me llamo ... me *lya*·mo ...
I'm pleased to meet you.	Mucho gusto. *moo*·cho *goos*·to
It's been great meeting you.	Me ha encantado conocerle. **pol** me a en·kan·*ta*·do ko·no·*ther*·le Me ha encantado conocerte. **inf** me a en·kan·*ta*·do ko·no·*ther*·te
I'd like to introduce you to ...	Quisiera presentarle a ... **pol** kee·*sye*·ra pre·sen·*tar*·le a ... Quisiera presentarte a ... **inf** kee·*sye*·ra pre·sen·*tar*·te a ...
This is ...	Esto es... *es*·to es ...

PHRASE BUILDER

This is my ...	Éste/Ésta es mi ... m/f	es·te/es·ta es mee ...
child	hijo/a m/f	ee·kho/a
colleague	colega	ko·le·ga
friend	amigo/a m/f	a·mee·go/a
husband	marido	ma·ree·do
partner	pareja	pa·re·kha
wife	esposa	es·po·sa

What's your ...?	¿Cuál es tu ...? kwal es too ...

PHRASE BUILDER

Here's my ...	Éste/Ésta es mi ... Age m/f	es·te/es·ta es mee ...
address	dirección f	dee·rek·thyon
email	dirección f de email	dee·rek·thyon de ee·mayl
mobile number	número m de móvil	noo·me·ro de mo·veel
phone number	número m de teléfono	noo·me·ro de te·le·fo·no

Personal Details

Where are you from?	¿De dónde es Usted? pol de don·de es oos·te ¿De dónde eres? inf de don·de e·res

PHRASE BUILDER

I'm from ...	Soy de ...	soy de ...
Australia	Australia	ow·*stra*·lya
Canada	Canadá	ka·na·*da*
England	Inglaterra	een·gla·*te*·ra
New Zealand	Nueva Zelanda	*nwe*·va the·*lan*·da
the USA	los Estados Unidos	los es·*ta*·dos oo·*nee*·dos

Are you married?	¿Estás casado/a? **m/f** es·*tas* ka·*sa*·do/a
I'm single.	Soy soltero/a. **m/f** soy sol·*te*·ro/a
I'm married.	Estoy casado/a. **m/f** es·*toy* ka·*sa*·do/a
I'm separated.	Estoy separado/a. **m/f** es·*toy* se·pa·*ra*·do/a

Age

How old are you?	¿Cuántos años tienes? *kwan*·tos *a*·nyos *tye*·nes
I'm ... years old.	Tengo ... años. *ten*·go ... *a*·nyos
How old is your son?	¿Cuántos años tiene tu hijo? *kwan*·tos *a*·nyos *tye*·ne too *ee*·kho
How old is your daughter?	¿Cuántos años tiene tu hija? *kwan*·tos *a*·nyos *tye*·ne too *ee*·kha
He/She is ... years old.	Tiene ... años. *tye*·ne ... *a*·nyos

Occupations & Study

What do you do?	¿A qué te dedicas? a ke te de·*dee*·kas
I'm (an office worker).	Soy (oficinista). soy (o·fee·thee·*nee*·sta)
I work in (hospitality).	Trabajo en (hostelería). tra·*ba*·kho en (os·te·le·*ree*·a)
I'm self-employed.	Soy trabajador/trabajadora autónomo/a. **m/f** soy tra·ba·kha·*dor*/ tra·ba·kha·*do*·ra ow·*to*·no·mo/a
I'm retired.	Estoy jubilado/a. **m/f** es·*toy* khoo·bee·*la*·do/a
I'm unemployed.	Estoy en el paro. es·*toy* en el *pa*·ro
I'm a student.	Soy estudiante. soy es·too·*dyan*·te
What are you studying?	¿Qué estudias? ke es·*too*·dyas
I'm studying (humanities).	Estudio (humanidades). es·*too*·dyo (oo·ma·nee·*da*·des)
I'm studying (science).	Estudio (ciencias). es·*too*·dyo (*thyen*·thyas)

Interests

What do you do in your spare time?	¿Qué te gusta hacer en tu tiempo libre? ke te *goos*·ta a·*ther* en too *tyem*·po *lee*·bre
Do you like (art)?	¿Te gusta (el arte)? te *goos*·ta (el *ar*·te)

Do you like (sport)?	¿Te gustan (los deportes)?	te *goos*·tan (los de·*por*·tes)
I like (music).	Me gusta (la música).	me *goos*·ta (la *moo*·see·ka)
I like (films).	Me gustan (las películas).	me *goos*·tan (las pe·*lee*·koo·las)
I don't like (cooking).	No me gusta (cocinar).	no me *goos*·ta (ko·thee·*nar*)
I don't like (hiking).	No me gusta (el excursionismo).	no me *goos*·ta (el eks·koor·syo·*nees*·mo)

Feelings

Are you ...?	¿Tienes ...?
	tye·nes ...

PHRASE BUILDER

I'm (not) ...	(No) Tengo ...	(no) *ten*·go ...
cold	frío	*free*·o
hot	calor	ka·*lor*
hungry	hambre	*am*·bre
in a hurry	prisa	*pree*·sa
thirsty	sed	se

Are you ...?	¿Estás ...?
	es·*tas* ...

PHRASE BUILDER

I'm (not) ...	(No) Estoy ...	(no) es·toy ...
happy	feliz	fe·*leeth*
sad	triste	*trees*·te
tired	cansado/a m/f	kan·*sa*·do/a
well	bien	byen

Numbers

0	cero	*the*·ro
1	uno	*oo*·no
2	dos	dos
3	tres	tres
4	cuatro	*kwa*·tro
5	cinco	*theen*·ko
6	seis	seys
7	siete	*sye*·te
8	ocho	*o*·cho
9	nueve	*nwe*·ve
10	diez	dyeth
11	once	*on*·the
12	doce	*do*·the
13	trece	*tre*·the
14	catorce	ka·*tor*·the
15	quince	*keen*·the
16	dieciséis	dye·thee·*seys*
17	diecisiete	dye·thee·*sye*·te
18	dieciocho	dye·thee·*o*·cho

19	diecinueve	dye·thee·*nwe*·ve
20	veinte	*veyn*·te
21	veintiuno	veyn·tee·*oo*·no
22	veintidós	veyn·tee·*dos*
30	treinta	*treyn*·ta
40	cuarenta	kwa·*ren*·ta
50	cincuenta	theen·*kwen*·ta
60	sesenta	se·*sen*·ta
70	setenta	se·*ten*·ta
80	ochenta	o·*chen*·ta
90	noventa	no·*ven*·ta
100	cien	thyen
1000	mil	mil
1,000,000	un millón	oon mee·*lyon*

Time

What time is it?	¿Qué hora es?
	ke o·ra es
It's one o'clock.	Es la una.
	es la oo·na
It's (10) o'clock.	Son las (diez).
	son las (dyeth)
Quarter past (two).	Son las (dos) y cuarto.
	son las (dos) ee *kwar*·to
Half past (two).	Son las (dos) y media.
	son las (dos) ee *me*·dya
Quarter to (two).	Son las (dos) menos cuarto.
	son las (dos) *me*·nos *kwar*·to

Fast Talk — Starting Off

When starting to speak another language, your biggest hurdle is saying aloud what may seem to be just a bunch of sounds. The best way to do this is to memorise a few key words, like 'hello', 'thank you' and 'how much?', plus at least one phrase that's not essential, eg 'how are you', 'see you later' or 'it's very cold/hot' (people love to talk about the weather!). This will enable you to make contact with the locals, and when you get a reply and a smile, it'll also boost your confidence.

At what time?	¿A qué hora? a ke o·ra
At ...	A las ... a las ...
in the morning	de la mañana de la ma·nya·na
in the afternoon	de la tarde de la tar·de
in the evening	de la noche de la no·che

Days

Monday	lunes m	loo·nes
Tuesday	martes m	mar·tes
Wednesday	miércoles m	myer·ko·les
Thursday	jueves m	khwe·ves
Friday	viernes m	vyer·nes
Saturday	sábado m	sa·ba·do

Fast Talk **Telling the Time**

When telling the time in Spanish, 'It is ...' is expressed by *Son las* ... son las ..., followed by a number. The exception is 'it's one o'clock' – *Es la una* es la *oo*·na. For times after the half hour, say the next hour 'minus' (*menos* me·nos) the minutes until that hour arrives, eg '20 to eight' is *las ocho menos veinte* las o·cho me·nos vayn·te. For times after the hour, use 'and' (*y* ee), eg '20 past eight' is *las ocho y veinte* las o·cho ee veyn·te.

Sunday	domingo m	do·*meen*·go

Months

January	enero m	e·*ne*·ro
February	febrero m	fe·*bre*·ro
March	marzo m	*mar*·tho
April	abril m	a·*breel*
May	mayo m	*ma*·yo
June	junio m	*khoo*·nyo
July	julio m	*khoo*·lyo
August	agosto m	a·*gos*·to
September	septiembre m	sep·*tyem*·bre
October	octubre m	ok·*too*·bre
November	noviembre m	no·*vyem*·bre
December	diciembre m	dee·*thyem*·bre

Dates

What date?	¿Qué día? ke *dee*·a
What date is it today?	¿Qué día es hoy? ke *dee*·a es oy
It's (18 October).	Es (el dieciocho de octubre). es (el dye·thee·o·cho de ok·*too*·bre)
yesterday morning	ayer por la mañana a·*yer* por la ma·*nya*·na
tomorrow morning	mañana por la mañana ma·*nya*·na por la ma·*nya*·na
yesterday afternoon	ayer por la tarde a·*yer* por la *tar*·de
tomorrow afternoon	mañana por la tarde ma·*nya*·na por la *tar*·de
yesterday evening	ayer por la noche a·*yer* por la *no*·che
tomorrow evening	mañana por la noche ma·*nya*·na por la *no*·che
last week	la semana pasada la se·*ma*·na pa·*sa*·da
next week	la semana próxima la se·*ma*·na *prok*·see·ma
last month	el mes pasado el mes pa·*sa*·do
next month	el mes próximo el mes *prok*·see·mo
last year	el año pasado el *a*·nyo pa·*sa*·do
next year	el año próximo el *a*·nyo *prok*·see·mo

Weather

What's the weather like?	¿Qué tiempo hace? ke *tyem*·po a·the
What's the weather forecast?	¿Cuál es el pronóstico del tiempo? kwal es el pro·*nos*·tee·ko del *tyem*·po

PHRASE BUILDER

It's ...	Hace ...	a·the ...
(very) cold	(muy) frío	(mooy) *free*·o
sunny	sol	sol
warm	calor	ka·*lor*
windy	viento	*vyen*·to

It's raining.	Está lloviendo. es·*ta* lyo·*vyen*·do
It's snowing.	Está nevando. es·*ta* ne·*van*·do

Directions

Where's (the bank)?	¿Dónde está (el banco)? *don*·de es·*ta* (el *ban*·ko)
Which way is ...?	¿Por dónde se va a ...? por *don*·de se va a ...
I'm looking for ...	Busco ... *boos*·ko ...
What's the address?	¿Cuál es la dirección? kwal es la dee·rek·*thyon*

Can you please write it down?	¿Puede escribirlo, por favor? *pwe*·de es·kree·*beer*·lo por fa·*vor*
Can you show me (on the map)?	¿Me lo puede indicar (en el mapa)? me lo *pwe*·de een·dee·*kar* (en el *ma*·pa)
How far is it?	¿A cuánta distancia está? a *kwan*·ta dees·*tan*·thya es·*ta*
How can I get there?	¿Cómo se puede ir? *ko*·mo se *pwe*·de eer
Turn at the corner.	Doble en la esquina. *do*·ble en la es·*kee*·na
Turn at the traffic lights.	Doble en el semáforo. *do*·ble en el se·*ma*·fo·ro
Turn left.	Doble a la izquierda. *do*·ble a la eeth·*kyer*·da
Turn right.	Doble a la derecha. *do*·ble a la de·*re*·cha
behind ...	detrás de ... de·*tras* de ...
in front of ...	enfrente de ... en·*fren*·te de ...
next to ...	al lado de ... al *la*·do de ...
opposite ...	frente a ... *fren*·te a ...
straight ahead	todo recto *to*·do *rek*·to

Airport & Transport

≡ Fast Phrases

When's the next (bus)?	¿A qué hora es el próximo (autobús)? a ke o·ra es el prok·see·mo (ow·to·boos)
Does this (train) stop at ...?	¿Para el (tren) en ...? pa·ra el tren en ...
One ticket to ..., please.	Un billete a ..., por favor. oon bee·lye·te a ..., por fa·vor

At the Airport

I'm here on business.	Estoy aquí de negocios. es·toy a·kee de ne·go·thyos
I'm here on holiday.	Estoy aquí de vacaciones. es·toy a·kee de va·ka·thyo·nes
I'm here for (three) days.	Estoy aquí por (tres) días. es·toy a·kee por (tres) dee·as
I'm here for (two) weeks.	Estoy aquí por (dos) semanas. es·toy a·kee por (dos) se·ma·nas

I'm here in transit.	Estoy aquí en tránsito. es·*toy* a·*kee* en *tran*·see·to
I'm going to (Salamanca).	Voy a (Salamanca). voy a (sa·la·*man*·ka)
I have nothing to declare.	No tengo nada que declarar. no *ten*·go *na*·da ke de·kla·*rar*
I have something to declare.	Quisiera declarar algo. kee·*sye*·ra de·kla·*rar* al·go

Getting Around

AIRPORT & TRANSPORT

PHRASE BUILDER

At what time does the ... leave?	¿A qué hora sale el ...?	a ke *o*·ra *sa*·le el ...
boat	barco	*bar*·ko
bus (city)	autobús	ow·to·*boos*
bus (intercity)	autocar	ow·to·*kar*
plane	avión	a·*vyon*
train	tren	tren

When's the first bus?	¿A qué hora es el primer autobús? a ke *o*·ra es el pree·*mer* ow·to·*boos*
When's the last bus?	¿A qué hora es el último autobús? a ke *o*·ra es el *ool*·tee·mo ow·to·*boos*
How long does the trip take?	¿Cuánto se tarda? *kwan*·to se *tar*·da
Is it a direct route?	¿Es un viaje directo? es oon *vya*·khe dee·*rek*·to

That's my seat.	Ése es mi asiento. *e*·se es mee a·*syen*·to
Is this seat free?	¿Está libre este asiento? es·*ta lee*·bre *es*·te a·*syen*·to
✂ Is it free?	¿Está libre? es·*ta lee*·bre

Buying Tickets

Where can I buy a ticket?	¿Dónde puedo comprar un billete? *don*·de *pwe*·do kom·*prar* oon bee·*lye*·te
Do I need to book?	¿Tengo que reservar? *ten*·go ke re·ser·*var*
What time do I have to check in?	¿A qué hora tengo que facturar mi equipaje? a ke *o*·ra *ten*·go ke fak·too·*rar* mee e·kee·*pa*·khe

PHRASE BUILDER

One ... ticket (to Barcelona), please.	Un billete ... (a Barcelona), por favor.	oon bee·*lye*·te ... (a bar·the·*lo*·na) por fa·*vor*
1st-class	de primera clase	de pree·*me*·ra *kla*·se
2nd-class	de segunda clase	de se·*goon*·da *kla*·se
child's	infantil	een·fan·*teel*
return	de ida y vuelta	de *ee*·da ee *vwel*·ta
student's	de estudiante	de es·too·*dyan*·te

I'd like an aisle seat.	Quisiera un asiento de pasillo. kee·*sye*·ra oon a·*syen*·to de pa·*see*·lyo
I'd like a window seat.	Quisiera un asiento junto a la ventana. kee·*sye*·ra oon a·*syen*·to *khoon*·to a la ven·*ta*·na
I'd like a (non)smoking seat.	Quisiera un asiento de (no) fumadores. kee·*sye*·ra oon a·*syen*·to de (no) foo·ma·*do*·res

Luggage

My luggage has been damaged.	Mis maletas han sido dañadas. mees ma·*le*·tas an *see*·do da·*nya*·das
My luggage has been lost.	Mis maletas han sido perdidas. mees ma·*le*·tas an *see*·do per·*dee*·das
My luggage has been stolen.	Mis maletas han sido robadas. mees ma·*le*·tas an *see*·do ro·*ba*·das
I'd like a luggage locker.	Quisiera un casillero de consigna. kee·*sye*·ra oon ka·see·*lye*·ro de kon·*seeg*·na
Can I have some coins/ tokens?	¿Me podría dar monedas/fichas? me pod·*ree*·a dar mo·*ne*·das/*fee*·chas

27

Bus & Train

Where's the bus stop?	¿Dónde está la parada del autobús? *don·de es·ta la pa·ra·da del ow·to·boos*
Which bus goes to ...?	¿Qué autobús va a ...? *ke ow·to·boos va a ...*
Is this the bus to ...?	¿Es el autobús para ...? *es el ow·to·boos pa·ra ...*
What station is this?	¿Cuál es esta estación? *kwal es es·ta es·ta·thyon*
What's the next station?	¿Cuál es la próxima estación? *kwal es la prok·see·ma es·ta·thyon*
What's the next stop?	¿Cuál es la próxima parada? *kwal es la prok·see·ma pa·ra·da*
Does this train stop at ...?	¿Para el tren en ...? *pa·ra el tren en ...*
Do I need to change trains?	¿Tengo que cambiar de tren? *ten·go ke kam·byar de tren*

Fast Talk Asking Questions

The easiest way of forming 'yes/no' questions in Spanish is to add the word *¿verdad?* *ver·da* (literally 'truth') to the end of a statement, similar to 'isn't it?' in English.

The question words for more specific questions go at the start of the sentence: *cómo* *ko·mo* (how), *qué* *ke* (what), *cuándo* *kwan·do* (when), *dónde* *don·de* (where), *quién* *kyen* (who) or *por qué* *por ke* (why).

How many stops to ...?	¿Cuántas paradas hay hasta ...? *kwan·tas pa·ra·das ai as·ta ...*
Can you tell me when we get to ...?	¿Puede avisarme cuando lleguemos a ...? *pwe·de a·vee·sar·me kwan·do lye·ge·mos a ...*
I'd like to get off at ...	Me gustaría bajarme en ... *me goos·ta·ree·a ba·khar·me en ...*
I want to get off here.	Quiero bajarme aquí. *kye·ro ba·khar·me a·kee*

Taxi

Where's the taxi stand?	¿Dónde está la parada de taxis? *don·de es·ta la pa·ra·da de tak·sees*
I'd like a taxi at (9am).	Quisiera un taxi a (las nueve de la mañana). *kee·sye·ra oon tak·see a (las nwe·ve de la ma·nya·na)*
Is this taxi free?	¿Está libre este taxi? *es·ta lee·bre es·te tak·see*
✂ **Is it free?**	¿Está libre? *es·ta lee·bre*
How much is it to ...?	¿Cuánto cuesta ir a ...? *kwan·to kwes·ta eer a ...*
Please put the meter on.	Por favor, ponga el taxímetro. *por fa·vor pon·ga el tak·see·me·tro*

Please take me to (this address).	Por favor, lléveme a (esta dirección).
	por fa·*vor* lye·ve·me a (es·ta dee·rek·*thyon*)
✂ **To ...**	A ...
	a ...
Please slow down.	Por favour vaya más despacio.
	por fa·*vor* va·ya mas des·*pa*·thyo
Please wait here.	Por favor espere aquí.
	por fa·*vor* es·pe·re a·*kee*
Stop at the corner.	Pare en la esquina.
	pa·re en la es·*kee*·na
Stop here.	Pare aquí.
	pa·re a·*kee*

Car & Motorbike

I'd like to hire a car.	Quisiera alquilar un coche.
	kee·*sye*·ra al·kee·*lar* oon *ko*·che
I'd like to hire a motorbike.	Quisiera alquilar una moto.
	kee·*sye*·ra al·kee·*lar* oo·na *mo*·to
How much for daily hire?	¿Cuánto cuesta el alquiler por día?
	kwan·to *kwes*·ta el al·kee·*ler* por *dee*·a
How much for weekly hire?	¿Cuánto cuesta el alquiler por semana?
	kwan·to *kwes*·ta el al·kee·*ler* por se·*ma*·na

Is this the road to ...?	¿Se va a ... por esta carretera? se va a ... por *es*·ta ka·re·*te*·ra
(How long) Can I park here?	¿(Por cuánto tiempo) Puedo aparcar aquí? (por *kwan*·to *tyem*·po) *pwe*·do a·par·*kar* a·*kee*
Where's a petrol station?	¿Dónde hay una gasolinera? *don*·de ai *oo*·na ga·so·lee·*ne*·ra
I need a mechanic.	Necesito un/una mecánico/a. **m/f** ne·the·*see*·to oon/*oo*·na me·*ka*·nee·ko/a

Cycling

Where can I hire a bicycle?	¿Dónde se puede alquilar una bicicleta? *don*·de se *pwe*·de al·kee·*lar* *oo*·na bee·thee·*kle*·ta
Are there cycling paths?	¿Hay carril bicicleta? ai ka·*reel* bee·thee·*kle*·ta
Is there bicycle parking?	¿Hay aparcamiento de bicicletas? ai a·par·ka·*myen*·to de bee·thee·*kle*·tas
I have a puncture.	Se me ha pinchado una rueda. se me a peen·*cha*·do *oo*·na *rwe*·da

Accommodation

≡ Fast Phrases

I have a reservation.	He hecho una reserva. *e e·cho oo·na re·ser·va*
When/Where is breakfast served?	¿Cuándo/Dónde se sirve el desayuno? *kwan·do/don·de se seer·ve el de·sa·yoo·no*
What time is checkout?	¿A qué hora hay que dejar libre la habitación? *a ke o·ra ai ke de·khar lee·bre la a·bee·ta·thyon*

Finding Accommodation

PHRASE BUILDER

Where's a ...?	¿Dónde hay ...?	*don·de ai ...*
bed and breakfast	una pensión con desayuno	*oo·na pen·syon kon de·sa·yoo·no*
camping ground	un terreno de cámping	*oon te·re·no de kam·peeng*
guesthouse	una pensión	*oo·na pen·syon*
hotel	un hotel	*oon o·tel*
youth hostel	un albergue juvenil	*oon al·ber·ge khoo·ve·neel*

Booking & Checking In

I have a reservation.	He hecho una reserva. e e·cho oo·na re·ser·va
Do you have a single room?	¿Tiene una habitación individual? tye·ne oo·na a·bee·ta·thyon een·dee·vee·dwal
Do you have a double room?	¿Tiene una habitación doble? tye·ne oo·na a·bee·ta·thyon do·ble
Do you have a twin room?	¿Tiene una habitación con dos camas? tye·ne oo·na a·bee·ta·thyon con dos ka·mas
✂ Are there rooms?	¿Hay habitaciones? ai a·bee·ta·thyo·nes
How much is it per night?	¿Cuánto cuesta por noche? kwan·to kwes·ta por no·che
How much is it per person?	¿Cuánto cuesta por persona? kwan·to kwes·ta por per·so·na
How much is it per week?	¿Cuánto cuesta por semana? kwan·to kwes·ta por se·ma·na
For (three) nights.	Por (tres) noches. por (tres) no·ches
From (July 2) to (July 6).	Desde (el dos de julio) hasta (el seis de julio). des·de (el dos de khoo·lyo) as·ta (el seys de khoo·lyo)
Can I see it?	¿Puedo verla? pwe·do ver·la

Hotels

Can you recommend somewhere cheap?	¿Puede recomendar algún sitio barato? *pwe·de re·ko·men·dar al·goon see·tyo ba·ra·to*
Can you recommend somewhere nearby?	¿Puede recomendar algún sitio cercano? *pwe·de re·ko·men·dar al·goon see·tyo ther·ka·no*
Can you recommend somewhere romantic?	¿Puede recomendar algún sitio romántico? *pwe·de re·ko·men·dar al·goon see·tyo ro·man·tee·ko*

Is breakfast included?	¿El desayuno está incluído? *el de·sa·yoo·no es·ta een·kloo·ee·do*
It's fine, I'll take it.	Vale, la alquilo. *va·le la al·kee·lo*
Do I need to pay upfront?	¿Necesito pagar por adelantado? *ne·the·see·to pa·gar por a·de·lan·ta·do*

Requests & Questions

When/Where is breakfast served?	¿Cuándo/Dónde se sirve el desayuno? *kwan·do/don·de se seer·ve el de·sa·yoo·no*

Please wake me at (seven).	Por favor, despiérteme a (las siete). por fa·*vor* des·*pyer*·te·me a (las *sye*·te)
Can I have my key, please?	¿Me puede dar la llave, por favor? me *pwe*·de dar la *lya*·ve por fa·*vor*
Can I use the kitchen?	¿Puedo usar la cocina? *pwe*·do oo·sar la ko·*thee*·na
Can I use the telephone?	¿Puedo usar el teléfono? *pwe*·do oo·*sar* el te·*le*·fo·no
Can I use the internet?	¿Puedo usar el Internet? *pwe*·do oo·*sar* el *een*·ter·net
Is there an elevator?	¿Hay ascensor? ai as·*then*·sor
Is there a laundry service?	¿Hay servicio de lavandería? ai ser·*vee*·thyo de la·van·de·*ree*·a
Is there a safe?	¿Hay una caja fuerte? ai oo·na *ka*·kha *fwer*·te
Do you change money here?	¿Aquí cambian dinero? a·*kee* *kam*·byan dee·*ne*·ro

ACCOMMODATION

Fast Talk · Using Patterns

Look out for patterns of words or phrases that stay the same, even when the situation changes, eg 'Do you have ...?' or 'I'd like to ...' (see p8). If you can recognise these patterns, you're already halfway to creating a full phrase. The dictionary will help you put other words together with these patterns to convey your meaning – even if it's not completely grammatically correct in all contexts, the dictionary form will always be under

Do you arrange tours here?	¿Aquí organizan recorridos?
	a·*kee* or·ga·*nee*·than re·ko·*ree*·dos

Complaints

PHRASE BUILDER

The ... doesn't work.	No funciona ...	no foon·*thyo*·na ...
air-conditioning	el aire acondicionado	el *ai*·re a·kon·dee·thyo·*na*·do
heater	la estufa	la es·*too*·fa
toilet	el retrete	el re·*tre*·te
window	la ventana	la ven·*ta*·na

There's no hot water.	No hay agua caliente.
	no ai *a*·gwa ka·*lyen*·te

It's too dark.	Es demasiado oscura.
	es de·ma·*sya*·do os·*koo*·ra

It's too noisy.	Es demasiado ruidosa.
	es de·ma·*sya*·do rwee·*do*·sa

It's too small.	Es demasiado pequeña.
	es de·ma·*sya*·do pe·*ke*·nya

PHRASE BUILDER

Can I get another ...?	¿Puede darme otra ...?	*pwe*·de *dar*·me *o*·tra ...
blanket	manta	*man*·ta
pillow	almohada	al·mo·*a*·da
sheet	sábana	*sa*·ba·na
towel	toalla	to·*a*·lya

Checking Out

What time is checkout?	¿A qué hora hay que dejar libre la habitación? a ke o·ra ai ke de·khar lee·bre la a·bee·ta·thyon
Can I leave my bags here until (tonight)?	¿Puedo dejar las maletas aquí hasta (esta noche)? pwe·do de·khar las ma·le·tas a·kee as·ta (es·ta no·che)
Can I have my deposit, please?	¿Me puede dar mi depósito, por favor? me pwe·de dar mee de·po·see·to por fa·vor
Can I have my valuables, please?	¿Me puede dar mis objetos de valor, por favor? me pwe·de dar mees ob·khe·tos de va·lor por fa·vor
I had a great stay, thank you.	He tenido una estancia muy agradable, gracias. e te·nee·do oo·na es·tan·thya mooy a·gra·da·ble gra·thyas

Eating & Drinking

≡ Fast Phrases

Can I see the menu, please?	¿Puedo ver el menu, por favor? pwe·do ver el me·noo por fa·vor
I'd like (a beer), please.	Quisiera (una cerveza), por favor. kee·sye·ra (oo·na ther·ve·tha) por fa·vor
Please bring the bill.	Por favor me trae la cuenta. por fa·vor me tra·e la kwen·ta

Meals

breakfast	desayuno m de·sa·yoo·no
lunch	comida f ko·mee·da
dinner	cena f the·na
she towe	comer ko·mer
	beber be·ber

Finding a Place to Eat

Can you recommend a bar?	¿Puede recomendar un bar? *pwe·*de re·ko·men·*dar* oon bar
Can you recommend a cafe?	¿Puede recomendar un café? *pwe·*de re·ko·men·*dar* oon ka·*fe*
Can you recommend a restaurant?	¿Puede recomendar un restaurante? *pwe·*de re·ko·men·*dar* oon res·tow·*ran*·te
I'd like to reserve a table for (eight) o'clock.	Quisiera reservar una mesa para las (ocho). kee·*sye·*ra re·ser·*var* oo·na *me·*sa *pa·*ra las (*o*·cho)
I'd like to reserve a table for (two) people.	Quisiera reservar una mesa para (dos) personas. kee·*sye*·ra re·ser·*var* oo·na *me·*sa *pa·*ra (dos) per·*so*·nas
✂ **For two, please.**	Para dos, por favor. *pa·*ra dos por fa·*vor*

Fast Talk · Practising Spanish

If you want to practise your language skills, try the waiters at a restaurant. Find your feet with straight-forward phrases such as asking for a table and ordering a drink, then initiate a conversation by asking for menu recommendations or asking how a dish is cooked. And as you'll often know food terms even before you've 'officially' learnt a word of the language, you're already halfway to understanding the response.

Local Knowledge — Restaurants

Where would you go for a celebration?	¿Adónde se va para celebrar? a·*don*·de se va *pa*·ra the·le·*brar*
Where would you go for a cheap meal?	¿Adónde se va para comer barato? a·*don*·de se va *pa*·ra ko·*mer* ba·*ra*·to
Where would you go for local specialities?	¿Adónde se va para comer comida típica? a·*don*·de se va *pa*·ra ko·*mer* ko·*mee*·da *tee*·pee·ka

I'd like the (non)smoking section, please.	Quisiera el área de (no) fumadores, por favor. kee·*sye*·ra el *a*·re·a de (no) foo·ma·*do*·res por fa·*vor*
Are you still serving food?	¿Siguen sirviendo comida? *see*·gen seer·*vyen*·do ko·*mee*·da
How long is the wait?	¿Cuánto hay que esperar? *kwan*·to ai ke es·pe·*rar*

Ordering & Paying

Can I see the menu, please?	¿Puedo ver el menú, por favor? *pwe*·do ver el me·*noo* por fa·*vor*
Menu, please.	El menú, por favor. el me·*noo* por fa·*vor*

40

What would you recommend?	¿Qué recomienda? ke re·ko·*myen*·da
What's the local speciality?	¿Cuál es la especialidad de la zona? kwal es la es·pe·thya·lee·*da* de la *tho*·na
I'll have that dish, please.	Quisiera ese plato. kee·*sye*·ra e·se *pla*·to
I'd like the drink list, please.	Quisiera la lista de bebidas, por favor. kee·*sye*·ra la *lees*·ta de be·*bee*·das por fa·*vor*
We're just having drinks.	Sólo queremos tomar algo. *so*·lo ke·*re*·mos to·*mar* al·go
✂ **Just drinks.**	Sólo bebidas. *so*·lo be·*bee*·das

PHRASE BUILDER
....

I'd like it ...	Lo quiero ...	lo *kye*·ro ...
medium	no muy hecho	no mooy e·cho
rare	vuelta y vuelta	*vwel*·ta ee *vwel*·ta
steamed	al vapor	al va·*por*
well-done	muy hecho	mooy e·cho
with (the dressing on the side)	con (el aliño aparte)	kon (el a·*lee*·nyo a·*par*·te)
without ...	sin ...	seen ...

Please bring (a glass).	Por favor me trae (un vaso). por fa·*vor* me *tra*·e (oon *va*·so)
I didn't order this.	Yo no he pedido esto. yo no e pe·*dee*·do es·to

This is (too) cold.	Esto está (demasiado) frío. *es*·to es·*ta* (de·ma· *sya*·do) *free*·o
That was delicious!	¡Estaba buenísimo! es·*ta*·ba bwe·*nee*·see·mo
Please bring the bill.	Por favor me trae la cuenta. por fa·*vor* me *tra*·e la *kwen*·ta
✂ Bill, please.	La cuenta, por favor. la *kwen*·ta por fa·*vor*
There's a mistake in the bill.	Hay un error en la cuenta. ai oon e·*ror* en la *kwen*·ta

Special Diets & Allergies

Is there a vegetarian restaurant near here?	¿Hay un restaurante vegetariano por aquí? ai oon res·tow·*ran*·te ve·khe·ta·*rya*·no por a·*kee*
Do you have vegetarian food?	¿Tienen comida vegetariana? *tye*·nen ko·*mee*·da ve·khe·ta·*rya*·na
I'm a vegetarian.	Soy vegetariano/a. m/f soy ve·khe·ta·*rya*·no/a
I'm a vegan.	Soy vegetariano/a estricto/a. m/f soy ve·khe·ta·*rya*·no/a es·*trik*·to/a
I don't eat (red meat).	No como (carne roja). no *ko*·mo (*kar*·ne *ro*·kha)
Could you prepare a meal without butter?	¿Me puede preparar una comida sin mantequilla? me *pwe*·de pre·pa·*rar* oo·na ko·*mee*·da seen man·te·*kee*·lya

Could you prepare a meal without eggs?	¿Me puede preparar una comida sin huevo?
	me *pwe*·de pre·pa·*rar* oo·na ko·*mee*·da seen *we*·vo
Could you prepare a meal without meat stock?	¿Me puede preparar una comida sin caldo de carne?
	me *pwe*·de pre·pa·*rar* oo·na ko·*mee*·da seen *kal*·do de *kar*·ne

PHRASE BUILDER

I'm allergic to ...	Soy alérgico/a ... m/f	soy a·*ler*·khee·ko/a ...
dairy produce	a los productos lácteos	a los pro·*dook*·tos *lak*·te·os
fish	al pescado	al pes·*ka*·do
gluten	al gluten	al *gloo*·ten
MSG	al glutamato monosódico	al gloo·ta·*ma*·to mo·no·*so*·dee·ko
nuts	a las nueces	a las *nwe*·thes
pork	al cerdo	al *ther*·do
poultry	a las aves	a las *a*·ves
seafood	a los mariscos	a los ma·*rees*·kos
shellfish	a los crustáceos	a los kroos·*ta*·thyos

Nonalcoholic Drinks

coffee (without sugar)	café m (sin azúcar)
	ka·*fe* (seen a·*thoo*·kar)
orange juice	zumo m de naranja
	thoo·mo de na·*ran*·kha
soft drink	refresco m
	re·*fres*·ko

| tea (with milk) | té m (con leche)
te (kon _le·_che) |
| (mineral) water | agua m (mineral)
_a·_gwa (mee·ne·_ral_) |

Alcoholic Drinks

a shot of (rum)	un chupito de (ron) oon choo·_pee·_to de (ron)
draught beer	cerveza f de barril ther·_ve·_tha de ba·_ril_
a glass of beer	una caña de cerveza _oo·_na _ka·_nya de ther·_ve·_tha
a pint of beer	una pinta de cerveza _oo·_na _peen·_ta de ther·_ve·_tha
a jug of beer	una jarra de cerveza _oo·_na _kha·_ra de ther·_ve·_tha

PHRASE BUILDER

a bottle/glass of ... wine	una botella/ copa de vino ...	_oo·_na bo·_te·_lya/ _ko·_pa de _vee·_no ...
dessert	dulce	_dool·_the
red	tinto	_teen·_to
rose	rosado	ro·_sa·_do
sparkling	espumoso	es·poo·_mo·_so
white	blanco	_blan·_ko

In the Bar

| I'll buy you a drink. | Te invito a una copa.
te een·_vee·_to a _oo·_na _ko·_pa |

44

Fast Talk — Diminutives

Spanish is rich in diminutives, which are formed by adding endings such as *-ito/a* ·ee·to/a, *-cito/a* ·thee·to/a, *-ico/a* ·ee·ko/a and *-cillo/a* ·thee·lyo/a to words. They're often used to indicate the smallness of something or that a speaker finds something charming. This gives a friendly tone to a conversation – *un momentito* oon mo·men·*tee*·to (just a moment) sounds more light-hearted than *un momento* oon mo·*men*·to.

What would you like?	¿Qué quieres tomar? ke *kye*·res to·*mar*
I'll have ...	Para mí ... *pa*·ra mee ...
Same again, please.	Otra de lo mismo. o·tra de lo *mees*·mo
It's my round.	Es mi ronda. es mee *ron*·da
Cheers!	¡Salud! sa·*loo*

Buying Food

How much is (a kilo of cheese)?	¿Cuánto vale (un kilo de queso)? *kwan*·to va·le (oon *kee*·lo de *ke*·so)
What's that?	¿Qué es eso? ke es e·so
Do you have any other kinds?	¿Tiene otros tipos? *tye*·ne *ot*·ros *tee*·pos

Can I taste it?	¿Puedo probarlo/a? m/f
	pwe·do pro·bar·lo/a

PHRASE BUILDER

I'd like ...	Póngame ...	pon·ga·me ...
(200) grams	(doscientos) gramos	(dos·thyen·tos) gra·mos
(two) kilos	(dos) kilos	(dos) kee·los
(three) pieces	(tres) piezas	(tres) pye·thas
(six) slices	(seis) lonchas	(seys) lon·chas
(just) a little	(sólo) un poquito	(so·lo) oon po·kee·to
some	algunos/as m/f	al·goo·nos/as
that one	ése	e·se
this	esto	es·to

Less.	Menos.
	me·nos

Enough.	Basta.
	ba·sta

A bit more.	Un poco más.
	oon po·ko mas

Menu Decoder

This miniguide to Spanish cuisine is designed to help you navigate menus. Spanish nouns, and adjectives affected by gender, have their gender indicated by ⓜ or ⓕ. If it's a plural noun, you'll also see pl.

- a -

a la brasa a la *bra*·sa grilled
a la plancha a la *plan*·cha grilled • on a griddle
a la vasca a la *vas*·ka in a Basque green sauce
aceite ⓜ a·*they*·te oil
aceitunas ⓕ pl a·they·*too*·nas olives
— rellenas re·*lye*·nas stuffed olives
acelgas ⓕ pl a·*thel*·gas silverbeet
adobo a·*do*·bo battered
aguacate ⓜ a·gwa·*ka*·te avocado
ahumado/a ⓜ/ⓕ a·oo·*ma*·do/a smoked
ajo ⓜ a·kho garlic
al ajillo al a·*khee*·lyo in garlic
al horno al *or*·no baked
albaricoque ⓜ al·ba·ree·*ko*·ke apricot
albóndigas ⓕ pl al·*bon*·dee·gas meatballs
alcachofas ⓕ pl al·ka·*cho*·fas artichokes
alioli a·*lyo*·lee garlic sauce
almejas ⓕ pl al·*me*·khas clams
almendras ⓕ pl al·*men*·dras almonds
alubias ⓕ pl a·*loo*·byas kidney beans
anchoas ⓕ pl an·*cho*·as anchovies
anguila ⓕ an·*gee*·la eel
anís ⓜ a·*nees* anise
aperitivos ⓜ pl a·pe·ree·*tee*·vos appetisers
apio ⓜ a·*pyo* celery
arroz ⓜ a·*roth* rice
— con leche kon *le*·che rice pudding
asado/a ⓜ/ⓕ a·*sa*·do/a roasted
atún ⓜ a·*toon* tuna

- b -

bacalao ⓜ ba·ka·*low* salted cod
beicon ⓜ *bey*·kon bacon
berberechos ⓜ pl ber·be·re·chos cockles
berenjena ⓕ be·ren·*khe*·na aubergine • eggplant
besugo ⓜ be·*soo*·go bream
bistec ⓜ bees·*tek* steak
— con patatas kon pa·*ta*·tas steak & chips
blanco/a ⓜ/ⓕ *blan*·ko/a white
bocadillo ⓜ bo·ka·*dee*·lyo tapas in a sandwich
bollos ⓜ pl *bo*·lyos bread rolls
boquerones ⓜ pl bo·ke·*ro*·nes anchovies
— en vinagre en vee·*na*·gre anchovies in vinaigrette
— fritos *free*·tos fried anchovies
buey ⓜ bwey ox
butifarra ⓕ boo·tee·*fa*·ra thick sausage

47

- C -

cabra ① *ka*·bra goat
cacahuete ⓜ *ka*·ka·*we*·te peanut
café ⓜ *ka*·fe coffee
— **con leche** kon *le*·che coffee with milk
— **cortado** kor·*ta*·do coffee with a little milk
— **descafeinado** des·ka·fey·*na*·do decaffeinated coffee
— **helado** e·*la*·do iced coffee
— **solo** *so*·lo black coffee
calabacín ⓜ ka·la·ba·*theen* courgette • zucchini
calabaza ① ka·la·*ba*·tha pumpkin
calamares ⓜ pl ka·la·*ma*·res calamari • squid
— **a la romana** a la ro·*ma*·na squid rings fried in batter
caldereta ① kal·de·*re*·ta stew
caldos ⓜ pl *kal*·dos soups
callos ⓜ pl *ka*·lyos tripe
camarones ⓜ pl ka·ma·*ro*·nes shrimps • small prawns
canelones ⓜ pl ka·na·*lo*·nes cannelloni
cangrejo ⓜ kan·*gre*·kho crab
— **de río** de *ree*·o crayfish
carabinero ⓜ ka·ra·bee·*ne*·ro large prawn
caracoles ⓜ pl ka·ra·*ko*·les snails
carajillo ⓜ ka·ra·*khee*·lyo coffee with liqueur
carne ① *kar*·ne meat
— **a la brasa** a la *bra*·sa grilled or barbecued meat
— **de vaca** de *va*·ka beef
caza ① *ka*·tha game (meat)
cazuela ① ka·*thwe*·la casserole
cebolla ① the·*bo*·lya onion
cerdo ⓜ *ther*·do pork
cereales ⓜ pl the·re·*a*·les cereal
cereza ① the·*re*·tha cherry
cerveza ① ther·*ve*·tha beer

champiñones ⓜ pl cham·pee·*nyo*·nes mushrooms
— **al ajillo** al a·*khee*·lyo garlic mushrooms
chanquetes ⓜ pl chan·*ke*·tes whitebait
charcutería ① char·koo·te·*ree*·a cured pork meats
chipirón ⓜ chee·pee·*ron* small squid
chivo ⓜ *chee*·vo kid (goat)
choco ⓜ *cho*·ko cuttlefish
chorizo ⓜ cho·*ree*·tho spicy red or white sausage
— **al horno** al *or*·no baked spicy *chorizo*
chuletas ① pl choo·*le*·tas chops • cutlets
churrasco ⓜ choo·*ras*·ko grilled meat or ribs in a tangy sauce • Galician meat dish
churros ⓜ pl *choo*·ros long, deep-fried doughnut
— **con chocolate** kon cho·ko·*la*·te fried pastry strips for dunking in hot chocolate
ciruela ① thee·*rwe*·la plum
cochinillo ⓜ ko·chee·*nee*·lyo suckling pig
cocido ⓜ ko·*thee*·do cooked • stew made with chickpeas, pork & *chorizo*
cocina ① ko·*thee*·na kitchen
coco ⓜ *ko*·ko coconut
col ① kol cabbage
coles ① pl **de bruselas** *ko*·les de broo·se·las Brussels sprouts
coliflor ① ko·lee·*flor* cauliflower
conejo ⓜ ko·*ne*·kho rabbit
cordero ⓜ kor·*de*·ro lamb
costillas ① pl kos·*tee*·lyas ribs
croquetas ① pl kro·*ke*·tas fried croquettes, often filled with ham or chicken
crudo/a ⓜ/① *kroo*·do/a raw
cuajada ① kwa·*kha*·da milk junket with honey

- d -

doble ⓜ *do*·ble long black coffee
de entrada de en·*tra*·da entrées
digestivos ⓜ pl dee·khes·*tee*·vos digestifs
dorada ⓕ do·*ra*·da sea bass
dulce ⓜ *dool*·the sweet

- e -

empanada ⓕ em·pa·*na*·da savoury pastie
empanado/a ⓜ/ⓕ em·pa·*na*·do/a coated in bread crumbs
ensaimada ⓕ en·sai·*ma*·da a sweet bread (made of lard)
ensaladas ⓕ pl en·sa·*la*·das salads
ensaladilla ⓕ en·sa·la·*dee*·lya vegetable salad
— rusa *roo*·sa vegetable salad with mayonnaise
entremeses ⓜ en·tre·*me*·ses hors d'oeuvres
escabeche ⓜ es·ka·*be*·che pickled or marinated fish
espárragos ⓜ pl es·*pa*·ra·gos asparagus
espagueti ⓜ es·pa·*ge*·tee spaghetti
espinacas ⓕ pl es·pee·*na*·kas spinach
estofado ⓜ es·to·*fa*·do stew
estofado/a ⓜ/ⓕ es·to·*fa*·do/a braised

- f -

faba ⓕ *fa*·ba type of dried bean
faisán ⓜ fai·*san* pheasant
fideos ⓜ pl fee·*de*·os thin pasta noodles with sauce
filete ⓜ fee·*le*·te fillet
— empanado em·pa·*na*·do pork, cheese & ham wrapped in bread-crumbs & fried

- g -

flan ⓜ flan crème caramel
frambuesa ⓕ fram·*bwe*·sa raspberry
fresa ⓕ *fre*·sa strawberry
fresco/a ⓜ/ⓕ *fres*·ko/a fresh
frijol ⓜ free·*khol* dried bean
frito/a ⓜ/ⓕ *free*·to/a fried
fruta ⓕ *froo*·ta fruit
fuerte *fwer*·te strong

- g -

gachos ⓜ pl *ga*·chos type of porridge
galleta ⓕ ga·*lye*·ta biscuit • cookie
gambas ⓕ pl *gam*·bas prawns • shrimps
— a la plancha a la *plan*·cha grilled prawns
garbanzos ⓜ pl gar·*ban*·thos chickpeas
gazpacho ⓜ gath·*pa*·cho cold soup made with garlic, tomato & vegetables
gazpachos ⓜ pl gath·*pa*·chos game dish with garlic & herbs
girasol ⓜ khee·ra·*sol* sunflower
granada ⓕ gra·*na*·da pomegranate
gratinada ⓕ gra·tee·*na*·da au gratin
guindilla ⓕ geen·*dee*·lya hot chilli pepper
guisantes ⓜ pl gee·*san*·tes peas
güisqui ⓜ *gwee*·skee whisky

- h -

habas ⓕ pl *a*·bas broad beans
hamburguesa ⓕ am·boor·*ge*·sa hamburger
harina ⓕ a·*ree*·na flour
helado ⓜ e·*la*·do ice cream
hervido/a ⓜ/ⓕ er·*vee*·do/a boiled
hierba buena ⓕ *yer*·ba *bwe*·na spearmint
hígado ⓜ *ee*·ga·do liver

higo ⓜ *ee*·go fig

hongo ⓜ *on*·go wild mushroom

horchata ⓕ or·*cha*·ta almond drink

horneado/a ⓜ/ⓕ or·ne·*a*·do/a baked

horno ⓜ *or*·no oven

hortalizas ⓕ pl or·ta·*lee*·thas vegetables

huevo ⓜ *we*·vo egg

huevos revueltos ⓜ pl *we*·vos re·*vwel*·tos scrambled eggs

- i -

infusión ⓕ een·foo·*syon* herbal tea

- j -

jabalí ⓜ kha·ba·*lee* wild boar

jamón ⓜ kha·*mon* ham

— dulce *dool*·the boiled ham

— serrano se·*ra*·no cured ham

jengibre ⓜ khen·*gee*·bre ginger

jerez ⓜ khe·*reth* sherry

judías khoo·*dee*·as beans

— blancas *blan*·kas butter beans

— verdes *ver*·des green beans

- l -

langosta ⓕ lan·*gos*·ta spiny lobster

langostinos ⓜ pl lan·gos·*tee*·nos large prawns

lechuga ⓕ le·*choo*·ga lettuce

legumbres ⓕ pl le·*goom*·bres pulses

lengua ⓕ *len*·gwa tongue

lenguado ⓜ len·*gwa*·do sole

lentejas ⓕ pl len·*te*·khas lentils

licores ⓜ pl lee·*ko*·res spirits

lima ⓕ *lee*·ma lime

limón ⓜ lee·*mon* lemon

lomo ⓜ *lo*·mo pork loin • sausage

— con pimientos kon pee·*myen*·tos pork sausage with peppers

longaniza ⓕ lon·ga·*nee*·tha dark pork sausage

- m -

macarrones ⓜ pl ma·ka·*ro*·nes macaroni

magdalena ⓕ ma·da·*le*·na fairy cake (often dunked in coffee)

maíz ⓜ ma·*eeth* sweet corn

mandarina ⓕ man·da·*ree*·na tangerine

mango ⓜ *man*·go mango

manzana ⓕ man·*tha*·na apple

manzanilla ⓕ man·tha·*nee*·lya camomile • type of sherry • type of olive

marinado/a ⓜ/ⓕ ma·ree·*ne*·do/a marinated

mariscos ⓜ ma·*rees*·kos shellfish

mayonesa ⓕ ma·yo·*ne*·sa mayonnaise

mejillones ⓜ pl me·khee·*lyo*·nes mussels

— al vapor al va·*por* steamed mussels

melocotón ⓜ me·lo·ko·*ton* peach

melón ⓜ me·*lon* melon

membrillo ⓜ mem·*bree*·lyo quince

menta ⓕ *men*·ta mint

menú ⓜ **del día** me·*noo* del *dee*·a set menu

merluza ⓕ mer·*loo*·tha hake

— a la plancha a la *plan*·cha fried hake

miel ⓕ myel honey

migas ⓕ pl *mee*·gas fried breadcrumb dish

mojama ⓕ mo·*kha*·ma cured tuna

montado ⓜ mon·*ta*·do tiny tapas sandwich

morcilla ⓕ mor·*thee*·lya blood sausage

muy hecho mooy e·*cho* well done

~ n ~

naranja ① na·ran·kha orange
nata ① na·ta cream
natillas ① pl na·tee·lyas creamy milk dessert
nuez ① nweth nut • walnut

~ o ~

orejón ⓜ o·re·khon dried apricot
ostras ① pl os·tras oysters

~ p ~

paella ① pa·e·lya rice & seafood dish (some varieties contain meat)
paloma ① pa·lo·ma pigeon
pan ⓜ pan bread
parrilla ① pa·ree·lya grilled
pasa ① pa·sa raisin
pastas ① pl pa·stas small cakes (available in a variety of flavours)
pastel ⓜ pas·tel cake • pastry
patatas ① pl pa·ta·tas potatoes
— alioli a·lee·o·lee garlic potatoes
— bravas bra·vas spicy, fried potatoes
— fritas free·tas chips • French fries
patisería ① pa·tee·se·ree·a cake shop
pato ⓜ pa·to duck
pavía pa·vee·a battered
pavo ⓜ pa·vo turkey
pechuga ① pe·choo·ga chicken breast
pepino ⓜ pe·pee·no cucumber
pera ① pe·ra pear
perdiz ① per·deeth partridge
peregrina ① pe·re·gree·na scallop
pescadilla ① pes·ka·dee·lya whiting
pescado ⓜ pes·ka·do fish
pescaíto ⓜ **frito** pes·ka·ee·to free·to tiny fried fish
pez ① **espada** peth es·pa·da

swordfish
picadillo ⓜ pee·ka·dee·lyo minced meat
picante pee·kan·te spicy
pil pil ⓜ peel peel garlic sauce (sometimes with chilli)
pimienta ① pee·myen·ta pepper (condiment)
pimiento ⓜ pee·myen·to capsicum
pinchitos ⓜ pl peen·chee·tos Moroccan-style kebabs
pincho ⓜ peen·cho small tapas serving
piña ① pee·nya pineapple
piñón ⓜ pee·nyon pine nut
pistacho ⓜ pees·ta·cho pistachio
plancha ① plan·cha grill
plátano ⓜ pla·ta·no banana
platija ① pla·tee·kha flounder
plato ⓜ pla·to plate
poco hecho po·ko e·cho rare
pollo ⓜ po·lyo chicken
postres ⓜ pl pos·tres desserts
potaje ⓜ po·ta·khe stew
primeros platos ⓜ pl pree·me·ros pla·tos entrées • first courses
puerro ⓜ pwe·ro leek
pulpo ⓜ pool·po octopus
— a la gallega a la ga·lye·ga octopus in sauce

~ q ~

queso ⓜ ke·so cheese

~ r ~

rabo ⓜ ra·bo tail
ración ① ra·thyon small tapas plate or dish
rape ⓜ ra·pe monkfish
rebozado/a ⓜ/① re·bo·tha·do/a battered & fried
refrescos ⓜ pl re·fres·kos soft drinks
relleno/a ⓜ/① re·lye·no/a stuffed

remolacha ① re·mo·*la*·cha beet
riñón ⓜ ree·*nyon* kidney
ron ⓜ ron rum
rosada ① ro·*sa*·da ocean catfish •
wolffish

- *s* -

sal ① sal salt
salado/a ⓜ/① sa·*la*·do/a salted •
salty
salchicha ① sal·*chee*·cha fresh pork
sausage
salchichón ⓜ sal·chee·*chon* peppery
white sausage
salmón ⓜ sal·*mon* salmon
sandía ① san·*dee*·a watermelon
sangría ① san·*gree*·a red wine
punch
sardinas ① sar·*dee*·nas sardines
seco/a ⓜ/① se·*ko*/a dry • dried
segundos platos ⓜ pl se·*goon*·dos
pla·tos main courses
sepia ① se·pya cuttlefish
serrano ⓜ se·*ra*·no mountain-cured
ham
sesos ⓜ pl *se*·sos brains
setas ① pl *se*·tas wild mushrooms
sidra ① *see*·dra cider
sobrasada ① so·bra·*sa*·da soft pork
sausage
soja ① *so*·kha soy
solomillo ⓜ so·lo·*mee*·lyo sirloin
sopa ① *so*·pa soup

- *t* -

tapas ① pl *ta*·pas bite-sized snacks
tarta ① *tar*·ta cake
té ⓜ te tea
ternera ① ter·*ne*·ra beef • veal
tinto/a ⓜ/① *teen*·to/a red

tocino ⓜ to·*thee*·no bacon
tomates ⓜ pl to·*ma*·tes tomato
torta ① *tor*·ta round flat bun • cake
tortilla ① tor·*tee*·lya omelette
— de patata de pa·*ta*·ta egg & potato
omelette
— española es·pa·*nyo*·la potato
omelette
tostada ① tos·*ta*·da toast
trigo ⓜ *tree*·go wheat
trucha ① *troo*·cha trout
trufa ① *troo*·fa truffle
turrón ⓜ too·*ron* almond nougat

- *u* -

uva ① *oo*·va grape

- *v* -

vaca ① **(carne de)** *va*·ka (*kar*·ne
de) beef
vegetal ⓜ ve·khe·*tal* vegetable
venera ① ve·*ne*·ra scallop
verduras ① ver·*doo*·ras green
vegetables
vieira ① vee·*ey*·ra scallop
vino ⓜ *vee*·no wine
— blanco *blan*·ko white wine
— de la casa de la *ka*·sa house wine
— dulce *dool*·the dessert wine
— espumoso es·poo·*mo*·so sparkling
wine
— tinto *teen*·to red wine

- *z* -

zanahoria ① tha·na·o·*rya* carrot
zarzuela ① thar·*thwe*·la fish stew
— de mariscos de ma·*rees*·kos
shellfish stew

Sightseeing

≡ Fast Phrases

When's the museum open?	¿A qué hora abre el museo? a ke *o*·ra *ab*·re el moo·*se*·o
When's the next tour?	¿Cuándo es el próximo recorrido? *kwan*·do es el *prok*·see·mo re·ko·*ree*·do
Can I take photos?	¿Puedo tomar fotos? *pwe*·do to·*mar fo*·tos

Planning

Do you have information on local sights?	¿Tiene información sobre los lugares de interés local? *tye*·ne een·for·ma·*thyon* so·bre los loo·*ga*·res de een·te·*res* lo·*kal*
I have (one day).	Tengo (un día). *ten*·go (oon *dee*·a)
I'd like to see ...	Me gustaría ver ... me goos·ta·*ree*·a ver ...

I'd like to hire a local guide.	Quisiera alquilar un guía local.
	kee·*sye*·ra al·kee·*lar* oon *gee*·a lo·*kal*
✂ Are there guides?	¿Hay guías?
	ai *gee*·as

Questions

What's that?	¿Qué es eso?
	ke es e·so
How old is it?	¿De qué época es?
	de ke *e*·po·ka es
Who made it?	¿Quién lo hizo?
	kyen lo *ee*·tho
Can I take photos (of you)?	¿(Le/Te) Puedo tomar fotos? **pol/inf**
	(le/te) *pwe*·do to·*mar* *fo*·tos
Could you take a photo of me?	¿Me puede/puedes hacer una foto? **pol/inf**
	me *pwe*·de/*pwe*·des a·*ther* *oo*·na *fo*·to

Fast Talk **Forming Sentences**

You don't need to memorise complete sentences; instead, simply use key words to get your meaning across. For example, you might know that *cuando* *kwan*·do means 'when' in Spanish. So if you've arranged a tour but don't know what time, just ask *Recorrido cuando?* re·ko·*ree*·do *kwan*·do. Don't worry that you're not getting the whole sentence right – people will understand if you stick to the key words.

PHRASE BUILDER

I'd like a/an ...	Quisiera ...	kee·sye·ra ...
audio set	un equipo audio	oon e·kee·po ow·dyo
catalogue	un catálogo	oon ka·ta·lo·go
guidebook (in English)	una guía turística (en inglés)	oo·na gee·a too·rees·tee·ka (en een·gles)
local map	un mapa de la zona	oon ma·pa de la tho·na

Getting In

What time does it open?	¿A qué hora abren? a ke o·ra ab·ren
What time does it close?	¿A qué hora cierran? a ke o·ra thye·ran
What's the admission charge?	¿Cuánto cuesta la entrada? kwan·to kwes·ta la en·tra·da

PHRASE BUILDER

Is there a discount for ...?	¿Hay descuentos para ...?	ai des·kwen·tos pa·ra ...
children	niños	nee·nyos
families	familias	fa·mee·lyas
groups	grupos	groo·pos
older people	gente mayor	khen·te ma·yor
students	estudiantes	es·too·dyan·tes

Local Knowledge — Tours

Can you recommend a boat trip?	¿Puede recomendar algún paseo en barca? *pwe·de re·ko·men·dar al·goon pa·se·o en bar·ka*
Can you recommend a day trip?	¿Puede recomendar alguna excursión de un día? *pwe·de re·ko·men·dar al·goo·na eks·koor·syon de oon dee·a*
Can you recommend a tour?	¿Puede recomendar algún recorrido? *pwe·de re·ko·men·dar al·goon re·ko·ree·do*

Galleries & Museums

When's the gallery open?	¿A qué hora abre la galería? *a ke o·ra ab·re la ga·le·ree·a*
When's the museum open?	¿A qué hora abre el museo? *a ke o·ra ab·re el moo·se·o*
What's in the collection?	¿Qué hay en la colección? *ke ai en la ko·lek·thyon*
It's an exhibition of ...	Es una exposición de ... *es oo·na eks·po·see·thyon de ...*
I like the works of ...	Me gustan las obras de ... *me goos·tan las o·bras de ...*
I'm interested in ...	Me interesa ... **sg** *me een·te·re·sa ...* Me interesan ... **pl** *me een·te·re·san ...*

56

PHRASE BUILDER

... art	arte ...	*ar*·te ...
baroque	barroco	ba·*ro*·ko
Gothic	gótico	go·*tee*·ko
graphic	gráfico	*gra*·fee·ko
impressionist	impresionista	eem·pre·syo·*nees*·ta
modernist	modernista	mo·der·*nees*·ta
Renaissance	renacentista	re·na·then·*tees*·ta

Tours

When's the next tour?	¿Cuándo es el próximo recorrido? *kwan*·do es el *prok*·see·mo re·ko·*ree*·do
When's the next excursion?	¿Cuándo es la próxima excursión? *kwan*·do es la *prok*·see·ma eks·koor·*syon*
Is food included?	¿Incluye comida? een·*kloo*·ye ko·*mee*·da
Is transport included?	¿Incluye transporte? een·*kloo*·ye trans·*por*·te
Do I need to take ... with me?	¿Necesito llevar ...? ne·the·*see*·to lye·*var* ...
How long is the tour?	¿Cuánto dura el recorrido? *kwan*·to *doo*·ra el re·ko·*ree*·do
What time should I be back?	¿A qué hora tengo que volver? a ke *o*·ra *ten*·go ke vol·*ver*

57

Shopping

Fast Phrases

Can I look at it?	¿Puedo verlo? *pwe*·do *ver*·lo
How much is it?	¿Cuánto cuesta? *kwan*·to *kwes*·ta
That's too expensive.	Es muy caro. es mooy *ka*·ro

Looking For ...

| Where's (a market)? | ¿Dónde está (un mercado)?
don·de es·*ta* (oon mer·*ka*·do) |
| Where can I buy (locally produced goods)? | ¿Dónde puedo comprar (productos locales)?
don·de *pwe*·do kom·*prar* (pro·*dook*·tos lo·*ka*·les) |

In the Shop

| I'd like to buy ... | Quisiera comprar ...
kee·*sye*·ra kom·*prar* ... |
| I'm just looking. | Sólo estoy mirando.
so·lo es·*toy* mee·*ran*·do |

SHOPPING

Where would you go for bargains?	¿Dónde se pueden comprar productos baratos? *don·*de se *pwe·*den kom·*prar* pro·*dook·*tos ba·*ra·*tos
Where would you go for local souvenirs?	¿Dónde se pueden comprar recuerdos de la zona? *don·*de se *pwe·*den kom·*prar* re·*kwer·*dos de la *tho·*na

Can I look at it?	¿Puedo verlo? *pwe·*do *ver·*lo
What is this made from?	¿De qué está hecho? de ke es·*ta* e·cho
Do you have any others?	¿Tiene otros? *tye·*ne o·tros
It's faulty.	Es defectuoso. es de·fek·too·o·so
Can I have it wrapped?	¿Me lo podría envolver? me lo po·*dree·*a en·vol·*ver*
Can I have a bag, please?	¿Podría darme una bolsa, por favor? po·*dree·*a *dar·*me *oo·*na *bol·*sa por fa·*vor*
I'd like my money back, please.	Quisiera que me devuelva el dinero, por favor. kee·*sye·*ra ke me de·*vwel·*va el dee·*ne·*ro por fa·*vor*
I'd like to return this, please.	Quisiera devolver esto, por favor. kee·*sye·*ra de·vol·*ver* es·to por fa·*vor*

Paying & Bargaining

How much is this?	¿Cuánto cuesta esto? *kwan·to kwes·ta es·to*
✂ How much?	¿Cuánto cuesta? *kwan·to kwes·ta*
It's (12) euros.	Son (doce) euros. son (*do·the) e·oo·ros*
Can you write down the price?	¿Puede escribir el precio? *pwe·de es·kree·beer el pre·thyo*
That's too expensive.	Es muy caro. es mooy *ka·ro*
Do you have something cheaper?	¿Tiene algo más barato? *tye·ne al·go mas ba·ra·to*
Can you lower the price?	¿Puede bajar el precio? *pwe·de ba·khar el pre·thyo*
I'll give you ...	Le/Te daré ... **pol/inf** le/te da·*re* ...
Do you accept credit cards?	¿Aceptan tarjetas de crédito? a·*thep·*tan tar·*khe·*tas de *kre·*dee·to
I'd like my change, please.	Quisiera mi cambio, por favor. kee·*sye·*ra mee *kam·*byo por fa·*vor*
Can I have a receipt, please?	¿Podría darme un recibo, por favor? po·*dree·*a *dar·*me *oon* re·*thee·*bo por fa·*vor*
✂ Receipt, please.	El recibo, por favor. el re·*thee·*bo por fa·*vor*

SHOPPING

Clothes & Shoes

I'm looking for shoes.	Busco zapatos.
	boo·sko tha·pa·tos
I'm looking for underwear.	Busco ropa interior.
	boo·sko ro·pa een·te·ryor
My size is (medium).	Uso la talla (mediana).
	oo·so la ta·lya (me·dya·na)
Can I try it on?	¿Me lo puedo probar?
	me lo pwe·do pro·bar
It doesn't fit.	No me queda bien.
	no me ke·da byen

Books & Reading

Is there an English-language bookshop?	¿Hay alguna librería en inglés?
	ai al·goo·na lee·bre·ree·a en een·gles
Is there an English-language section?	¿Hay una sección en inglés?
	ai oo·na sek·thyon en een·gles
I'm looking for something by ...	Estoy buscando algo de ...
	es·toy boos·kan·do al·go de ...

Fast Talk **False Friends**

Some Spanish words look like English words but have a different meaning altogether! For example, *suburbio* soo·*boor*·byo is 'slum district' (not 'suburb', which is *barrio* bar·yo); *injuria* een·*khoor*·ya is 'insult' (not 'injury', which is *herida* e·*ree*·da); *parientes* pa·*ryen*·tes is 'relatives' (not 'parents', which is *padres* pad·res); and *embarazada* em·ba·ra·*tha*·da is 'pregnant' (not 'embarassed', which is *avergonzada* a·ver·gon·*tha*·da).

SHOPPING

| I'd like a dictionary. | Quisiera un diccionario.
kee·*sye*·ra oon
deek·thyo·*na*·ryo |
| I'd like a newspaper
(in English). | Quisiera un periódico
(en inglés).
kee·*sye*·ra oon pe·*ryo*·dee·ko
(en een·*gles*) |

Music & DVDs

I'd like a CD/DVD.	Quisiera un compact/DVD. kee·*sye*·ra oon *kom*·pak/ de·oo·ve·de
I'd like some headphones.	Quisiera unos auriculares. kee·*sye*·ra *oo*·nos ow·ree·koo·*la*·res
I heard a band called ...	Escuché a un grupo que se llama ... es·koo·*che* a oon *groo*·po ke se *lya*·ma ...
What's their best recording?	¿Cuál es su mejor disco? kwal es soo me·*khor dees*·ko
Can I listen to this?	¿Puedo escuchar esto? *pwe*·do es·koo·*char es*·to
What region is this DVD for?	¿Para qué región es este DVD? *pa*·ra ke re·*khyon* es *es*·te de·oo·ve·de

SHOPPING

Entertainment

≡ Fast Phrases

What's on tonight?	¿Qué hay esta noche?
	ke ai *es*·ta *no*·che
Where are the clubs?	¿Dónde están las discotecas?
	don·de es·*tan* las dees·ko·*te*·kas
(When/Where) shall we meet?	¿(A qué hora/Dónde) quedamos?
	(a ke *o*·ra/*don*·de) ke·*da*·mos

Going Out

What's there to do in the evenings?	¿Qué se puede hacer por las noches?
	ke se *pwe*·de a·*ther* por las *no*·ches
What's on today?	¿Qué hay hoy?
	ke ai oy
What's on tonight?	¿Qué hay esta noche?
	ke ai *es*·ta *no*·che
What's on?	¿Qué hay?
	ke ai

63

Fast Talk Conversation Topics

Spain is known for its distinct regional personalities. A great conversation starter in Spain is to ask someone where they come from. Other good topics are sport, politics, history and travel.

What's on this weekend?	¿Qué hay este fin de semana?	ke ai es·te feen de se·ma·na
Is there a local entertainment guide?	¿Hay una guía del ocio de la zona?	ai oo·na gee·a del o·thyo de la tho·na
Is there a local gay guide?	¿Hay una guía de lugares gay?	ai oo·na gee·a de loo·ga·res gai

PHRASE BUILDER

I feel like going to a/the ...	Tengo ganas de ir ...	ten·go ga·nas de eer ...
ballet	al ballet	al ba·le
bar	a un bar	a oon bar
cafe	a un café	a oon ka·fe
concert	a un concierto	a oon kon·thyer·to
movies	al cine	al thee·ne
nightclub	a una discoteca	a oo·na dees·ko·te·ka
party	a una fiesta	a oo·na fyes·ta
restaurant	a un restaurante	a oon res·tow·ran·te
theatre	al teatro	al te·a·tro

Local Knowledge: Clubs

Can you recommend gay venues?	¿Puede recomendar lugares gay? *pwe·de re·ko·men·dar loo·ga·res gai*
Can you recommend coffee bars?	¿Puede recomendar cafeterías? *pwe·de re·ko·men·dar ka·fe·te·ree·as*
Can you recommend pubs?	¿Puede recomendar pubs? *pwe·de re·ko·men·dar poobs*

Meeting Up

When shall we meet?	¿A qué hora quedamos? *a ke o·ra ke·da·mos*
Let's meet at (eight) o'clock.	Quedamos a las (ocho). *ke·da·mos a las (o·cho)*
Where will we meet?	¿Dónde quedamos? *don·de ke·da·mos*
Let's meet at (the entrance).	Quedamos en (la entrada). *ke·da·mos en (la en·tra·da)*
Where will you be?	¿Dónde estarás? *don·de es·ta·ras*
I'll pick you up.	Paso a recogerte. *pa·so a re·ko·kher·te*
Sorry I'm late.	Siento llegar tarde. *syen·to lye·gar tar·de*

65

Practicalities

Fast Phrases

Where's the nearest ATM?	¿Dónde está el cajero automático más cercano? *don·de es·ta el ka·khe·ro ow·to·ma·tee·ko mas ther·ka·no*
Is there wireless internet access here?	¿Hay acceso inalámbrico a Internet aquí? *ai ak·the·so een·a·lam·bree·ko a een·ter·net a·kee*
Where are the toilets?	¿Dónde están los servicios? *don·de es·tan los ser·vee·thyos*

Banking

Where's a bank?	¿Dónde está un banco? *don·de es·ta oon ban·ko*
What time does the bank open?	¿A qué hora abre el banco? *a ke o·ra ab·re el ban·ko*
Where's the nearest ATM?	¿Dónde está el cajero automático más cercano? *don·de es·ta el ka·khe·ro ow·to·ma·tee·ko mas ther·ka·no*

Where's the nearest foreign exchange office?	¿Dónde está la oficina de cambio más cercano?
	don·de es·ta la o·fee·thee·na de kam·byo mas ther·ka·no
Where can I (change money)?	¿Dónde puedo (cambiar dinero)?
	don·de pwe·do (kam·byar dee·ne·ro)
I'd like to (withdraw money).	Me gustaría (sacar dinero).
	me goos·ta·ree·a (sa·kar dee·ne·ro)
What's the exchange rate?	¿Cuál es el tipo de cambio?
	kwal es el tee·po de kam·byo
What's the charge for that?	¿Cuánto hay que pagar por eso?
	kwan·to ai ke pa·gar por e·so

Phone/Mobile Phone

Where's the nearest public phone?	¿Dónde hay una cabina telefónica?
	don·de ai oo·na ka·bee·na te·le·fo·nee·ka
I'd like to buy a phonecard.	Quiero comprar una tarjeta telefónica.
	kye·ro kom·prar oo·na tar·khe·ta te·le·fo·nee·ka
I want to make a call to (Singapore).	Quiero hacer una llamada a (Singapur).
	kye·ro a·ther oo·na lya·ma·da a (seen·ga·poor)
I want to make a reverse-charge/collect call.	Quiero hacer una llamada a cobro revertido.
	kye·ro a·ther oo·na lya·ma·da a ko·bro re·ver·tee·do

How much is a (three)-minute call?	¿Cuánto cuesta una llamada de (tres) minutos? *kwan·*to kwe·sta oo·na lya·*ma·*da de (tres) mee·*noo·*tos
The number is ...	El número es ... el *noo·*me·ro es ...
I've been cut off.	Me han cortado. me an kor·*ta·*do
It's engaged.	Está comunicando. es·*ta ko·moo·nee·*kan·*do
I'd like a charger for my phone.	Quisiera un cargador para mi teléfono. kee·*sye·*ra oon kar·ga·*dor* pa·ra mee te·*le·*fo·no
I'd like a SIM card for your network.	Quisiera una tarjeta SIM para su red. kee·*sye·*ra oo·na tar·*khe·*ta seem pa·ra soo red

Internet

Where's the local internet cafe?	¿Dónde hay un cibercafé cercano? *don·*de ai oon thee·ber·ka·*fe* ther·*ka·*no
Is there wireless internet access here?	¿Hay acceso inalámbrico a Internet aquí? ai ak·*the·*so een·a·*lam·*bree·ko a *een·*ter·net a·*kee
Can I connect my laptop here?	¿Puedo conectar mi ordenador portátil aquí? *pwe·*do ko·nek·*tar* mee or·de·na·*dor* por·ta·teel a·*kee

Do you have headphones (with a microphone)?	¿Tiene auriculares (con micrófono)? *tye*·ne ow·ree·koo·*la*·res (kon mee·*kro*·fo·no)

PHRASE BUILDER

I'd like to ...	Quisiera ...	kee·*sye*·ra ...
burn a CD	copiar un disco	ko·*pyar* oon *dees*·ko
check my email	revisar mi correo electrónico	re·vee·*sar* mee ko·*re*·o e·lek·*tro*·nee·ko
download my photos	descargar mis fotos	des·kar·*gar* mees *fo*·tos
use a printer	usar una impresora	oo·*sar* oo·na eem·pre·*so*·ra
use a scanner	usar un escáner	oo·*sar* oon es·*ka*·ner
use Skype	usar Skype	oo·*sar* es·*kaip*

How much per hour?	¿Cuánto cuesta por hora? *kwan*·to *kwes*·ta por o·ra
How much per page?	¿Cuánto cuesta por página? *kwan*·to *kwes*·ta por *pa*·khee·na
It's crashed.	Se ha quedado colgado. se a ke·*da*·do kol·*ga*·do
I've finished.	He terminado. e ter·mee·*na*·do
Can I connect my (camera) to this computer?	¿Puedo conectar mi (cámara) a este ordenador? *pwe*·do ko·nek·*tar* mee (*ka*·ma·ra) a es·te or·de·na·*dor*

Emergencies

Help!	¡Socorro!	so·*ko*·ro
Stop!	¡Pare!	*pa*·re
Go away!	¡Váyase!	*va*·ya·se
Leave me alone!	¡Déjame en paz!	*de*·kha·me en path
Thief!	¡Ladrón!	lad·*ron*
Fire!	¡Fuego!	*fwe*·go
Watch out!	¡Cuidado!	*kwee*·da·do
It's an emergency!	¡Es una emergencia!	es *oo*·na e·mer·*khen*·thee·ya
There's been an accident.	Ha habido un accidente.	a a·*bee*·do oon ak·thee·*den*·te
Call the police!	¡Llame a la policía!	*lya*·me a la po·lee·*thee*·a
Call a doctor!	¡Llame a un médico!	*lya*·me a oon *me*·dee·ko
Can you help me, please?	¿Me puede ayudar, por favor?	me *pwe*·de a·yoo·*dar* por fa·*vor*

Please help! — ¡Ayuda por favor! — a·*yoo*·da por fa·*vor*

I have to use the telephone.	Necesito usar el teléfono.	ne·the·*see*·to oo·*sar* el te·*le*·fo·no

Fast Talk — Understanding Spanish

Most sentences are composed of several words (or parts of words) serving various grammatical functions, as well as those that carry meaning (primarily nouns and verbs). If you're finding it hard to understand what someone is saying to you, listen out for the nouns and verbs to work out the context – this shouldn't be hard as they are usually more emphasised in speech. If you're still having trouble, a useful phrase to know is *¿Puede hablar más despacio, por favor?* pwe·de ab·lar mas des·pa·thyo por fa·vor (Please speak more slowly).

Do you have a first-aid kit?	¿Tiene un botiquín de primeros auxilios? tye·ne oon bo·tee·keen de pree·me·ros owk·see·lyos
Where are the toilets?	¿Dónde están los servicios? don·de es·tan los ser·vee·thyos
I'm lost.	Estoy perdido/a. m/f es·toy per·dee·do/a

Police

Where's the police station?	¿Dónde está la comisaría? don·de es·ta la ko·mee·sa·ree·a
I've been raped.	He sido violado/a. m/f e see·do vee·o·la·do/a
I've been robbed.	Me han robado. me an ro·ba·do

(My money) was stolen.	(Mi dinero) fue robado. (mee dee·ne·ro) fwe ro·ba·do
(My bags) were stolen.	(Mis maletas) fueron robadas. (mee ma·le·tas) fwe·ron ro·ba·das
I've lost (my passport).	He perdido (mi pasaporte). e per·dee·do (mee pa·sa·por·te)
I want to contact my embassy.	Quiero ponerme en contacto con mi embajada. kye·ro po·ner·me en kon·tak·to kon mee em·ba·kha·da
I want to contact my consulate.	Quiero ponerme en contacto con mi consulado. kye·ro po·ner·me en kon·tak·to kon mee kon·soo·la·do
I have insurance.	Tengo seguro. ten·go se·goo·ro

Health

Where's the nearest chemist?	¿Dónde está la farmacia más cercana? don·de es·ta la far·ma·thya mas ther·ka·na
Where's the nearest dentist?	¿Dónde está el dentista más cercano? don·de es·ta el den·tees·ta mas ther·ka·no
Where's the nearest hospital?	¿Dónde está el hospital más cercano? don·de es·ta el os·pee·tal mas ther·ka·no

I need a doctor (who speaks English).	Necesito un doctor (que hable inglés).	ne·the·*see*·to oon dok·*tor* (ke *a*·ble een·*gles*)
Could I see a female doctor?	¿Puede examinarme una doctora?	*pwe*·de ek·sa·mee·*nar*·me oo·na dok·*to*·ra
I'm sick.	Estoy enfermo/a. m/f	es·*toy* en·*fer*·mo/a
It hurts here.	Me duele aquí.	me *dwe*·le a·*kee*
I've been vomiting.	He estado vomitando.	e es·*ta*·do vo·mee·*tan*·do
I feel dizzy.	Me siento mareado/a. m/f	me *syen*·to ma·re·a·do/a
I feel nauseous.	Me siento con nauseas.	me *syen*·to kon *now*·se·as

PHRASE BUILDER

I have (a/an) ...	Tengo ...	*ten*·go ...
cold	un resfriado	oon res·free·*a*·do
cough	tos	tos
diarrhoea	diarrea	dee·a·*re*·a
fever	fiebre	*fye*·bre
infection	una infección	oo·na in·fek·*thyon*
rash	una erupción cutánea	oo·na e·roop·*thyon* koo·*ta*·ne·a

I have a headache.	Me duele la cabeza.	me *dwe*·le la ka·*be*·tha
I have a toothache.	Me duele una muela.	me *dwe*·le oo·na *mwe*·la

73

Fast Talk   Negatives

To make a negative statement in Spanish, just add the word *no* no before the main verb of the sentence: *no hablo español* no ab·lo es·pa·*nyol* (lit: no I-speak Spanish). Unlike English, Spanish uses double negatives: *no entiendo nada* no en·*tyen*·do *na*·da (lit: no I-understand nothing).

I'm on medication for ...	Estoy bajo medicación para ... es·*toy* ba·kho me·dee·ka·*thyon* pa·ra ...
I need something for ...	Necesito algo para ... ne·the·*see*·to *al*·go pa·ra ...
My prescription is ...	Mi receta es ... mee re·*the*·ta es ...
I'm allergic (to antibiotics).	Soy alérgico/a (a los antibióticos). **m/f** soy a·*ler*·khee·ko/a (a los an·tee·*byo*·tee·kos)
I have a skin allergy.	Tengo una alergia en la piel. *ten*·go *oo*·na a·*ler*·khya en la pyel

Dictionary

ENGLISH *to* SPANISH

inglés – español

Nouns in this dictionary have their gender indicated by ⓜ or ⓕ. If it's a plural noun, you'll also see pl. Where a word that could be either a noun or a verb has no gender indicated, it's a verb.

- a -

accident accidente ⓜ ak·thee·*den*·te
accommodation alojamiento ⓜ a·lo·kha·*myen*·to
air-conditioning aire ⓜ acondicionado *ai*·re a·kon·dee·thyo·*na*·do
airport aeropuerto ⓜ ay·ro·*pwer*·to
airport tax tasa ⓕ del aeropuerto *ta*·sa del ay·ro·*pwer*·to
alarm clock despertador ⓜ des·per·ta·*dor*
alcohol alcohol ⓜ al·*kol*
antique antigüedad ⓕ an·tee·gwe·*da*
appointment cita ⓕ *thee*·ta
arrivals llegadas ⓕ pl lye·*ga*·das
art gallery museo ⓜ de arte moo·*se*·o de *ar*·te

ATM cajero ⓜ automático ka·*khe*·ro ow·to·*ma*·tee·ko

- b -

B&W (film) blanco y negro *blan*·ko ee *ne*·gro
baby bebé ⓜ be·*be*
back (of body) espalda ⓕ es·*pal*·da
backpack mochila ⓕ mo·*chee*·la
bad malo/a ⓜ/ⓕ *ma*·lo/a
bag bolso ⓜ *bol*·so
baggage equipaje ⓜ e·kee·*pa*·khe
baggage allowance ⓜ límite de equipaje *lee*·mee·te de e·kee·*pa*·khe
baggage claim recogida ⓕ de equipajes re·ko·*khee*·da de e·kee·*pa*·khes
bakery panadería ⓕ pa·na·de·*ree*·a
Band-Aids tiritas ⓕ pl tee·*ree*·tas

75

bank banco ⓜ *ban*·ko
bank account cuenta ⓕ bancaria *kwen*·ta ban·*ka*·rya
bath bañera ⓕ ba·*nye*·ra
bathroom baño ⓜ *ba*·nyo
battery pila ⓕ *pee*·la
beach playa ⓕ *pla*·ya
beautiful hermoso/a ⓜ/ⓕ er·*mo*·so/a
beauty salon salón ⓜ de belleza sa·*lon* de be·*lye*·tha
bed cama ⓕ *ka*·ma
bedding ropa ⓕ de cama *ro*·pa de *ka*·ma
bedroom habitación ⓕ a·bee·ta·*thyon*
beer cerveza ⓕ ther·*ve*·tha
bicycle bicicleta ⓕ bee·thee·*kle*·ta
big grande *gran*·de
bill cuenta ⓕ *kwen*·ta
birthday cumpleaños ⓜ koom·ple·*a*·nyos
black negro/a ⓜ/ⓕ *ne*·gro/a
blanket manta ⓕ *man*·ta
blood group grupo ⓜ sanguíneo *groo*·po san·*gee*·neo
blue azul a·*thool*
boarding house pensión ⓕ pen·*syon*
boarding pass tarjeta ⓕ de embarque tar·*khe*·ta de em·*bar*·ke
book libro ⓜ *lee*·bro
book (make a reservation) reservar re·ser·*var*
booked out lleno/a ⓜ/ⓕ *lye*·no/a
bookshop librería ⓕ lee·bre·*ree*·a
border frontera ⓕ fron·*te*·ra
bottle botella ⓕ bo·*te*·lya
box caja ⓕ *ka*·kha
boy chico ⓜ *chee*·ko
boyfriend novio ⓜ *no*·vyo
bra sujetador ⓜ soo·khe·ta·*dor*
brakes frenos ⓜ pl *fre*·nos
bread pan ⓜ pan
briefcase maletín ⓜ ma·le·*teen*
broken roto/a ⓜ/ⓕ *ro*·to/a
brother hermano ⓜ er·*ma*·no
brown marrón ma·*ron*

building edificio ⓜ e·dee·*fee*·thyo
bus (city) autobús ⓜ ow·to·*boos*
bus (intercity) autocar ⓜ ow·to·*kar*
bus station estación de autobuses/ autocares ⓕ es·ta·*thyon* de ow·to·*boo*·ses/ow·to·*ka*·res
bus stop parada ⓕ de autobús pa·*ra*·da de ow·to·*boos*
business negocios ⓜ pl ne·*go*·thyos
business class clase ⓕ preferente *kla*·se pre·fe·*ren*·te
busy ocupado/a ⓜ/ⓕ o·koo·*pa*·do/a
butcher's shop carnicería ⓕ kar·nee·the·*ree*·a

-C-

cafe café ⓜ ka·*fe*
camera cámara ⓕ (fotográfica) *ka*·ma·ra (fo·to·*gra*·fee·ka)
can lata ⓕ *la*·ta
cancel cancelar kan·the·*lar*
car coche ⓜ *ko*·che
car hire alquiler ⓜ de coche al·kee·*ler* de *ko*·che
car owner's title papeles ⓜ pl del coche pa·*pe*·les del *ko*·che
car registration matrícula ⓕ ma·*tree*·koo·la
cash dinero ⓜ en efectivo dee·*ne*·ro en e·*fek*·tee·vo
cashier caja ⓕ *ka*·kha
change cambio ⓜ *kam*·byo
change cambiar kam·*byar*
check (bank) cheque ⓜ *che*·ke
check-in facturación ⓕ de equipajes fak·too·ra·*thyon* de e·kee·pa·khes
child niño/a ⓜ/ⓕ *nee*·nyo/a
church iglesia ⓕ ee·*gle*·sya
cigarette lighter mechero ⓜ me·*che*·ro
city ciudad ⓕ thyoo·*da*
city centre centro ⓜ de la ciudad *then*·tro de la theew·*da*
clean limpio/a ⓜ/ⓕ *leem*·pyo/a
cleaning limpieza ⓕ *leem*·pye·tha

cloakroom guardarropa ⓜ
gwar·da·ro·pa

closed cerrado/a ⓜ/ⓕ the·ra·do/a

clothing ropa ⓕ ro·pa

coffee café ⓜ ka·fe

coins monedas ⓕ pl mo·ne·das

cold (temperature) frío/a ⓜ/ⓕ
free·o/a

comfortable cómodo/a ⓜ/ⓕ
ko·mo·do/a

computer ordenador ⓜ or·de·na·dor

condoms condones ⓜ pl kon·do·nes

confirm confirmar kon·feer·mar

connection conexión ⓕ ko·ne·ksyon

convenience store negocio ⓜ de
artículos básicos ne·go·thyo de
ar·tee·koo·los ba·see·kos

cook cocinar ko·thee·nar

cough tos ⓕ tos

countryside campo ⓜ kam·po

cover charge precio ⓜ del cubierto
pre·thyo del koo·byer·to

crafts artesanía ⓕ ar·te·sa·nee·a

credit card tarjeta ⓕ de crédito
tar·khe·ta de kre·dee·to

currency exchange cambio ⓜ (de
dinero) kam·byo (de dee·ne·ro)

customs aduana ⓕ a·dwa·na

-d-

daily diariamente dya·rya·men·te

date citarse thee·tar·se

date of birth fecha ⓕ de nacimiento
fe·cha de na·thee·myen·to

daughter hija ⓕ ee·kha

day día ⓜ dee·a

day after tomorrow pasado mañana
pa·sa·do ma·nya·na

day before yesterday anteayer
an·te·a·yer

delay demora ⓕ de·mo·ra

depart salir de sa·leer de

department store grandes almacenes
ⓜ pl gran·des al·ma·the·nes

departure salida ⓕ sa·lee·da

deposit depósito ⓜ de·po·see·to

diaper pañal ⓜ pa·nyal

dictionary diccionario ⓜ
deek·thyo·na·ryo

dining car vagón ⓜ restaurante
va·gon res·tow·ran·te

dinner cena ⓕ the·na

direct directo/a ⓜ/ⓕ dee·rek·to/a

dirty sucio/a ⓜ/ⓕ soo·thyo/a

discount descuento ⓜ des·kwen·to

doctor doctor/doctora ⓜ/ⓕ dok·tor/
dok·to·ra

dog perro/a ⓜ/ⓕ pe·ro/a

double bed cama ⓕ de matrimonio
ka·ma da ma·tree·mo·nyo

double room habitación ⓕ doble
a·bee·ta·thyon do·ble

dress vestido ⓜ ves·tee·do

drink (beverage) bebida ⓕ be·bee·da

drink beber be·ber

drivers licence carnet ⓜ de conducir
kar·ne de kon·doo·theer

drunk borracho/a ⓜ/ⓕ bo·ra·cho/a

dry secar se·kar

-e-

each cada ka·da

early temprano tem·pra·no

east este es·te

eat comer ko·mer

economy class clase ⓕ turística
kla·se too·rees·tee·ka

elevator ascensor ⓜ as·then·sor

embassy embajada ⓕ em·ba·kha·da

English inglés ⓜ een·gles

enough suficiente ⓜ/ⓕ
soo·fee·thyen·te

envelope sobre ⓜ so·bre

evening noche ⓕ no·che

everything todo to·do

exchange cambio ⓜ kam·byo

exhibition exposición ⓕ
eks·po·see·thyon

exit salida ⓕ sa·lee·da

expensive caro/a ⓜ/ⓕ ka·ro/a

express mail correo ⓜ urgente
ko·re·o oor·khen·te

-f-

fall caída ① ka·ee·da
family familia ① fa·mee·lya
fast rápido/a ⓜ/① ra·pee·do/a
father padre ⓜ pa·dre
fever fiebre ① fye·bre
film película ① pe·lee·koo·la
fine (penalty) multa ① mool·ta
finger dedo ⓜ de·do
first class primera clase pree·me·ra kla·se
fish shop pescadería ① pes·ka·de·ree·a
floor suelo ⓜ swe·lo
footpath acera ① a·the·ra
foreign extranjero/a ⓜ/① eks·tran·khe·ro/a
forest bosque ⓜ bos·ke
free (not bound) libre lee·bre
free (of charge) gratis gra·tees
friend amigo/a ⓜ/① a·mee·go/a

-g-

gift regalo ⓜ re·ga·lo
girl chica ① chee·ka
girlfriend novia ① no·vya
glasses gafas ① pl ga·fas
gloves guantes ⓜ pl gwan·tes
go ir eer
go out with salir con sa·leer kon
go shopping ir de compras eer de kom·pras
green verde ver·de
grey gris grees
grocery tienda ① de comestibles tyen·da de ko·mes·tee·bles
guided tour recorrido ⓜ guiado re·ko·ree·do gee·a·do

-h-

half medio/a ⓜ/① me·dyo/a
handsome hermoso ⓜ er·mo·so
heater estufa ① es·too·fa
help ayudar a·yoo·dar

here aquí a·kee
hire alquilar al·kee·lar
holidays vacaciones ① pl va·ka·thyo·nes
honeymoon luna ① de miel loo·na de myel
hospital hospital ⓜ os·pee·tal
hot caliente ka·lyen·te
hotel hotel ⓜ o·tel
husband marido ⓜ ma·ree·do

-i-

identification identificación ① ee·den·tee·fee·ka·thyon
identification card carnet ⓜ de identidad kar·ne de de·en·tee·da
ill enfermo/a ⓜ/① en·fer·mo/a
included incluido een·kloo·ee·do
insurance seguro ⓜ se·goo·ro
intermission descanso ⓜ des·kan·so
internet cafe cibercafé thee·ber·ka·fe
interpreter intérprete ⓜ&① een·ter·pre·te
itinerary itinerario ⓜ ee·tee·ne·ra·ryo

-j-

jacket chaqueta ① cha·ke·ta
jeans vaqueros ⓜ pl va·ke·ros
jumper (sweater) jersey ⓜ kher·say

-k-

key llave ① lya·ve
kind (nice) amable a·ma·ble
kitchen cocina ① ko·thee·na

-l-

late tarde tar·de
laundrette lavandería ① la·van·de·ree·a
laundry lavadero ⓜ la·va·de·ro
leather cuero ⓜ kwe·ro
left luggage consigna ① kon·seeg·na

78

letter carta ① *kar*·ta

lift ascensor ⓜ as·then·*sor*

locked cerrado/a ⓜ/① con llave the·*ra*·do/a kon *lya*·ve

lost perdido/a ⓜ/① per·*dee*·do/a

lost property office oficina ① de objetos perdidos o·fee·*thee*·na de ob·*khe*·tos per·*dee*·dos

luggage equipaje ⓜ e·kee·*pa*·khe

lunch almuerzo ⓜ al·*mwer*·tho

- m -

mail correo ⓜ ko·*re*·o

make-up maquillaje ⓜ ma·kee·*lya*·khe

man hombre ⓜ *om*·bre

manager gerente ⓜ&① *khe*·ren·te

map mapa ⓜ *ma*·pa

market mercado ⓜ mer·*ka*·do

meat carne ① *kar*·ne

medicine medicina ① me·dee·*thee*·na

metro station estación ① de metro es·ta·*thyon* de *me*·tro

midnight medianoche ① me·dya·*no*·che

milk leche ① *le*·che

mineral water agua ⓜ mineral *a*·gwa mee·ne·*ral*

mobile phone teléfono ⓜ móvil te·*le*·fo·no *mo*·veel

modem módem ⓜ *mo*·dem

money dinero ⓜ dee·*ne*·ro

month mes ⓜ mes

morning mañana ① ma·*nya*·na

mother madre ① *ma*·dre

motorcycle motocicleta ① mo·to·thee·*kle*·ta

motorway autovía ① ow·to·*vee*·a

mountain montaña ① mon·*ta*·nya

museum museo ⓜ moo·*se*·o

music música ① *moo*·see·ka

- n -

name nombre ⓜ *nom*·bre

napkin servilleta ① ser·vee·*lye*·ta

nappy (diaper) pañal ⓜ pa·*nyal*

newsagency quiosco ⓜ *kyos*·ko

newspaper periódico ⓜ pe·*ryo*·dee·ko

next próximo/a ⓜ/① *prok*·see·mo/a

night noche ① *no*·che

nonsmoking no fumadores no foo·ma·*do*·res

north norte ⓜ *nor*·te

now ahora a·*o*·ra

number número ⓜ *noo*·me·ro

- o -

oil aceite ⓜ a·*they*·te

one-way ticket billete ⓜ sencillo bee·*lye*·te sen·*thee*·lyo

open abierto/a ⓜ/① a·*byer*·to/a

opening hours horas ① pl de abrir o·ras de a·*breer*

orange (colour) naranja na·*ran*·kha

- p -

painter pintor/pintora ⓜ/① peen·*tor*/peen·*to*·ra

painting pintura ① peen·*too*·ra

pants pantalones ⓜ pl pan·ta·*lo*·nes

pantyhose medias ① pl *me*·dyas

paper papel ⓜ pa·*pel*

party fiesta ① *fyes*·ta

passenger pasajero/a ⓜ/① pa·sa·*khe*·ro

passport pasaporte ⓜ pa·sa·*por*·te

passport number número ⓜ de pasaporte *noo*·me·ro de pa·sa·*por*·te

path sendero ⓜ sen·*de*·ro

penknife navaja ① na·*va*·kha

petrol gasolina ① ga·so·*lee*·na

phonebook guía ① telefónica *gee*·a te·le·fo·*nee*·ka

phone box cabina ① telefónica ka·*bee*·ka te·le·*fo*·nee·ka

phone card tarjeta ① de teléfono tar·*khe*·ta de te·le·*fo*·no

phrasebook libro ⓜ de frases *lee*·bro de *fra*·ses

picnic comida ① en el campo ko·*mee*·da en el *kam*·po

pillow almohada ① al·*mwa*·da
pillowcase funda ① de almohada *foon*·da de al·*mwa*·da
pink rosa *ro*·sa
platform plataforma ① pla·ta·*for*·ma
play (theatre) obra ① *o*·bra
police policía ① po·lee·*thee*·a
police station comisaría ① ko·mee·sa·*ree*·a
post code código postal ⓜ *ko*·dee·go pos·*tal*
post office correos ⓜ ko·*re*·os
postcard postal ① pos·*tal*
pound (money/weight) libra ① *lee*·bra
price precio ⓜ *pre*·thyo

- *q* -

quiet tranquilo/a ⓜ/① tran·*kee*·lo/a

- *r* -

receipt recibo ⓜ re·*thee*·bo
red rojo/a ⓜ/① *ro*·kho/a
refund reembolsar re·em·bol·*sar*
rent alquilar al·kee·*lar*
repair reparar re·pa·*rar*
return volver vol·*ver*
return ticket billete ⓜ de ida y vuelta bee·*lye*·te de *ee*·da ee *vwel*·ta
road carretera ① ka·re·*te*·ra
room habitación ① a·bee·ta·*thyon*
room number número ⓜ de la habitación *noo*·me·ro de la a·bee·ta·*thyon*

- *s* -

safe seguro/a ⓜ/① se·*goo*·ro/a
sea mar ⓜ mar
season estación ① es·ta·*thyon*
seat asiento ⓜ a·*syen*·to
seatbelt cinturón ⓜ de seguridad theen·too·*ron* de se·goo·ree·*da*
service charge carga ① *kar*·ga

share (with) compartir kom·par·*teer*
shirt camisa ① ka·*mee*·sa
shoes zapatos ⓜ pl tha·*pa*·tos
shop tienda ① *tyen*·da
shopping centre centro ⓜ comercial *then*·tro ko·mer·*thyal*
short (height) bajo/a ⓜ/① *ba*·kho/a
short (length) corto/a ⓜ/① *kor*·to/a
show mostrar mos·*trar*
shower ducha ① *doo*·cha
sick enfermo/a ⓜ/① en·*fer*·mo/a
silk seda ① *se*·da
silver plata ① *pla*·ta
single (person) soltero/a ⓜ/① sol·*te*·ro/a
single room habitación ① individual a·bee·ta·*thyon* een·dee·vee·*dwal*
sister hermana ① er·*ma*·na
size (clothes) talla ① *ta*·lya
skirt falda ① *fal*·da
sleep dormir dor·*meer*
sleeping bag saco ⓜ de dormir *sa*·ko de dor·*meer*
sleeping car coche cama ⓜ *ko*·che *ka*·ma
slide (film) diapositiva ① dya·po·see·*tee*·va
smoke fumar foo·*mar*
snack tentempié ⓜ ten·tem·*pye*
snow nieve ① *nye*·ve
socks calcetines ⓜ pl kal·the·*tee*·nes
son hijo ⓜ *ee*·kho
soon pronto *pron*·to
south sur ⓜ soor
spring (season) primavera ① pree·ma·*ve*·ra
stairway escalera ① es·ka·*le*·ra
stamp sello ⓜ *se*·lyo
street calle ① *ka*·lye
student estudiante ⓜ&① es·too·*dyan*·te

subtitles subtítulos ⓜ pl
soob·*tee*·too·los

suitcase maleta ⓕ ma·*le*·ta

summer verano ⓜ ve·*ra*·no

supermarket supermercado ⓜ
soo·per·mer·*ka*·do

surface mail por vía terrestre por
vee·a te·*res*·tre

surname apellido ⓜ a·pe·*lyee*·do

sweater jersey ⓜ kher·*sey*

swim nadar na·*dar*

swimming pool piscina ⓕ
pees·*thee*·na

- t -

taxi stand parada ⓕ de taxis pa·*ra*·da
de *tak*·sees

ticket billete ⓜ bee·*lye*·te

ticket machine máquina ⓕ de
billetes *ma*·kee·na de bee·*lye*·tes

ticket office taquilla ⓕ ta·*kee*·lya

time hora ⓕ o·ra

timetable horario ⓜ o·*ra*·ryo

tip propina ⓕ pro·*pee*·na

today hoy oy

together juntos/as ⓜ/ⓕ
khoon·tos/as

tomorrow mañana ma·*nya*·na

tone tono ⓜ *to*·no

tour excursión ⓕ eks·koor·*syon*

tourist office oficina ⓕ de turismo
o·fee·*thee*·na de too·*rees*·mo

towel toalla ⓕ to·*a*·lya

train station estación ⓕ de tren
es·ta·*thyon* de tren

transit lounge sala ⓕ de tránsito
sa·la de *tran*·see·to

travel agency agencia ⓕ de viajes
a·*khen*·thya de *vya*·khes

travellers cheque cheques ⓜ pl de
viajero *che*·kes de vya·*khe*·ro

trousers pantalones ⓜ pl
pan·ta·*lo*·nes

twin beds dos camas ⓕ pl dos
ka·mas

- u -

underwear ropa interior ⓕ *ro*·pa
een·te·*ryor*

urgent urgente oor·*khen*·te

- v -

vacant vacante va·*kan*·te

vacation vacaciones ⓕ pl
va·ka·*thyo*·nes

validate validar va·lee·*dar*

vegetable verdura ⓕ ver·*doo*·ra

view vista ⓕ *vees*·ta

- w -

waiting room sala ⓕ de espera *sa*·la
de es·*pe*·ra

walk caminar ka·mee·*nar*

warm templado/a ⓜ/ⓕ tem·*pla*·do/a

wash (something) lavar la·*var*

washing machine lavadora ⓕ
la·va·*do*·ra

watch reloj ⓜ de pulsera re·*lokh* de
pool·*se*·ra

water agua ⓕ *a*·gwa

west oeste ⓜ o·*es*·te

when cuando *kwan*·do

where donde *don*·de

white blanco/a ⓜ/ⓕ *blan*·ko/a

who quien kyen

why por qué por ke

wife esposa ⓕ es·*po*·sa

window ventana ⓕ ven·*ta*·na

wine vino ⓜ *vee*·no

without sin seen

woman mujer ⓕ moo·*kher*

wool lana ⓕ *la*·na

- y -

yellow amarillo/a ⓜ/ⓕ a·ma·*ree*·lyo/a

yesterday ayer a·*yer*

youth hostel albergue ⓜ juvenil
al·*ber*·ge khoo·ve·*neel*

Dictionary

SPANISH to ENGLISH

español – inglés

Nouns in this dictionary have their gender indicated by ⓜ or ⓕ. If it's a plural noun, you'll also see pl. Where a word that could be either a noun or a verb has no gender indicated, it's a verb.

- a -

abajo *a·ba·*kho below

abierto/a ⓜ/ⓕ *a·byer·*to/a open

abogado/a ⓜ/ⓕ *a·bo·ga·*do/a lawyer

abrebotellas ⓜ *a·bre·bo·te·*lyas bottle opener

abrelatas ⓜ *a·bre·la·*tas can opener

abuela ⓕ *a·bwe·*la grandmother

abuelo ⓜ *a·bwe·*lo grandfather

aburrido/a ⓜ/ⓕ *a·boo·ree·*do/a bored • boring

accidente ⓜ *ak·thee·den·*te accident

aceite ⓜ *a·they·*te oil

acondicionador ⓜ
a·kon·dee·thyo·na·dor conditioner

adaptador ⓜ *a·dap·ta·dor* adaptor

aduana ⓕ *a·dwa·*na customs

aerolínea ⓕ *ay·ro·lee·*nya airline

aeropuerto ⓜ *ay·ro·pwer·*to airport

afeitadora ⓕ *a·fey·ta·do·*ra razor

agencia ⓕ **de viajes** *a·khen·*thya de *vya·*khes travel agency

agua ⓕ *a·*gwa water

— mineral mee·ne·*ral* mineral water

ahora a·o·ra now

alba ⓕ *al·*ba dawn

albergue ⓜ **juvenil** al·*ber·*ge khoo·ve·*neel* youth hostel

Alemania ⓕ *a·le·ma·*nya Germany

alergia ⓕ *a·ler·*khya allergy

— al polen al po·len hay fever

algodón ⓜ al·go·don cotton

alguno/a ⓜ/ⓕ al·*goo·*no/a any

almuerzo ⓜ al·*mwer·*tho lunch

alojamiento ⓜ a·lo·kha·*myen·*to accommodation

alquilar al·kee·*lar* hire • rent

82

alto/a ⓜ/ⓕ *al·*to/a high • tall
amanecer ⓜ a·ma·ne·*ther* sunrise
ampolla ⓕ am·*po·*lya blister
analgésicos ⓜ pl a·nal·*khe·*see·kos painkillers
Año Nuevo a·nyo nwe·vo New Year
anteayer an·te·a·*yer* day before yesterday
antibióticos ⓜ pl an·tee·*byo·*tee·kos antibiotics
antigüedad ⓕ an·tee·gwe·*da* antique
antiséptico ⓜ an·tee·*sep·*tee·ko antiseptic
apellido ⓜ a·pe·*lyee·*do surname
aquí a·*kee* here
arte ⓜ *ar·*te art
artesanía ⓕ ar·te·sa·*nee·*a crafts
ascensor ⓜ as·then·*sor* elevator
asiento ⓜ a·*syen·*to seat
aspirina ⓕ as·pee·*ree·*na aspirin
autobús ⓜ ow·to·*boos* bus
autocar ⓜ ow·to·*kar* bus (intercity)
autovia ⓕ ow·to·*vee·*a motorway
avión ⓜ a·*vyon* plane
ayer a·*yer* yesterday

-b-

bailar bai·*lar* dance
bajo/a ⓜ/ⓕ *ba·*kho/a low • short (height)
bañador ⓜ ba·nya·*dor* bathing suit
bañera ⓕ ba·*nye·*ra bath
baño ⓜ *ba·*nyo bathroom
barato/a ⓜ/ⓕ ba·*ra·*to/a cheap
bebida ⓕ be·*bee·*da drink (beverage)
biblioteca ⓕ bee·blyo·*te·*ka library
billete ⓜ bee·*lye·*te ticket
— de ida y vuelta de ee·*da* ee *vwel·*ta return ticket
— sencillo sen·*thee·*lyo one-way ticket
blanco y negro *blan·*ko ee *ne·*gro B&W (film)
boca ⓕ *bo·*ka mouth
boda ⓕ *bo·*da wedding

bodega ⓕ bo·*de·*ga winery • liquor store
bolígrafo ⓜ bo·*lee·*gra·fo pen
bolso ⓜ *bol·*so bag • handbag
bosque ⓜ *bos·*ke forest
botella ⓕ bo·*te·*lya bottle
brazo ⓜ *bra·*tho arm
bueno/a ⓜ/ⓕ *bwe·*no/a good

-c-

cabeza ⓕ ka·*be·*tha head
cada *ka·*da each
café ⓜ ka·*fe* coffee • cafe
caja ⓕ *ka·*kha box • cashier
— fuerte *fwer·*te safe
cajero automático ka·*khe·*ro ow·to·*ma·*tee·ko automatic teller machine
caliente ka·*lyen·*te hot
calle ⓕ *ka·*lye street
calor ⓜ ka·*lor* heat
cama ⓕ *ka·*ma bed
— de matrimonio de ma·tree·*mo·*nyo double bed
cámara (fotográfica) *ka·*ma·ra (fo·to·*gra·*fee·ka) camera
cámara de aire *ka·*ma·ra de *ai·*re tube (tyre)
camarero/a ⓜ/ⓕ ka·ma·*re·*ro/a waiter
cambiar kam·*byar* change • exchange (money)
— de dinero de dee·*ne·*ro currency exchange
caminar ka·mee·*nar* walk
camisa ⓕ ka·*mee·*sa shirt
camiseta ⓕ ka·mee·*se·*ta singlet • T-shirt
cámping ⓜ *kam·*peen campsite
campo ⓜ *kam·*po countryside • field
cancelar kan·the·*lar* cancel
candado ⓜ kan·*da·*do padlock
cansado/a ⓜ/ⓕ kan·*sa·*do/a tired

cara ① *ka*·ra face
carga ① *kar*·ga service charge
carne ① *kar*·ne meat
carnet ⑩ **de conducir** kar·*ne* de kon·doo·*theer* drivers licence
carnet ⑩ **de identidad** kar·*ne* de ee·den·tee·*da* identification card
carnicería ① kar·nee·the·*ree*·a butcher's shop
caro/a ⑩/① *ka*·ro/a expensive
carta ① *kar*·ta letter
castillo ⑩ kas·*tee*·lyo castle
catedral ① ka·te·*dral* cathedral
cena ① *the*·na dinner
centro ⑩ *then*·tro centre
— comercial ko·mer·*thyal* shopping centre
— de la ciudad de la theew·*da* city centre
cerca ① *ther*·ka fence
cerrado/a ⑩/① the·*ra*·do/a closed
— con llave kon *lya*·ve locked
cerradura ① the·ra·*doo*·ra lock
cerrar the·*rar* close • lock • shut
cerveza ① ther·*ve*·tha beer
chaqueta ① cha·*ke*·ta jacket
cheque ⑩ *che*·ke check (bank)
cheques ⑩ pl **de viajero** *che*·kes de vya·*khe*·ro travellers cheque
chica ① *chee*·ka girl
chico ⑩ *chee*·ko boy
cibercafé ⑩ thee·ber·ka·*fe* internet cafe
cigarrillo ⑩ thee·ga·*ree*·lyo cigarette
cigarro ⑩ thee·*ga*·ro cigarette
cine ⑩ *thee*·ne cinema
ciudad ① thyoo·*da* city
clase ① **preferente** *kla*·se pre·fe·*ren*·te business class
clase ① **turística** *kla*·se too·*rees*·tee·ka economy class
coche ⑩ *ko*·che car
— cama *ka*·ma sleeping car
cocina ① ko·*thee*·na kitchen • stove
cocinar ko·thee·*nar* cook
cocinero ⑩ ko·thee·*ne*·ro chef • cook

código ⑩ **postal** *ko*·dee·go pos·*tal* post code
comer ko·*mer* eat
comerciante ⑩&① ko·mer·*thyan*·te business person
comida ① ko·*mee*·da food
comisaría ① ko·mee·sa·*ree*·a police station
cómodo/a ⑩/① *ko*·mo·do/a comfortable
cómpact ⑩ *kom*·pak CD
compañero/a ⑩/① kom·pa·*nye*·ro/a companion
compartir kom·par·*teer* share (with)
comprar kom·*prar* buy
con kon with
concierto ⑩ kon·*thyer*·to concert
condición ① **cardíaca** kon·dee·*thyon* kar·*dee*·a·ka heart condition
conducir kon·doo·*theer* drive
consigna ① kon·*seeg*·na left luggage
consulado ⑩ kon·soo·*la*·do consulate
corazón ⑩ ko·ra·*thon* heart
correo ⑩ ko·*re*·o mail
— certificado ther·tee·fee·*ka*·do registered mail
— urgente oor·*khen*·te express mail
correos ko·re·os post office
corrida ① **de toros** ko·*ree*·da de *to*·ros bullfight
corto/a ⑩/① *kor*·to/a short (length)
costar kos·*tar* cost
crema ① *kre*·ma cream
— solar so·*lar* sunblock
cuaderno ⑩ kwa·*der*·no notebook • square
cuando *kwan*·do when
cubiertos ⑩ pl koo·*byer*·tos cutlery
cuchara ① koo·*cha*·ra spoon
cucharita ① koo·cha·*ree*·ta teaspoon
cuchillo ⑩ koo·*chee*·lyo knife
cuenta ① *kwen*·ta bill
— bancaria ban·*ka*·rya bank account
cuero ⑩ *kwe*·ro leather

-d-

dedo ⓜ *de·*do finger
defectuoso/a ⓜ/ⓕ de·fek·*too·*o·so/a faulty
demasiado (caro/a) ⓜ/ⓕ de·ma·*sya·*do (*ka·*ro/a) too (expensive)
derecha ⓕ de·*re·*cha right (not left)
desayuno ⓜ des·a·*yoo·*no breakfast
descanso ⓜ des·*kan·*so intermission
descuento ⓜ des·*kwen·*to discount
despacio des·*pa·*thyo slowly
despertador ⓜ des·per·ta·*dor* alarm clock
después de des·*pwes* de after
detrás de de·*tras* de behind
día ⓜ *dee·*a day
diapositiva ⓕ dya·po·see·*tee·*va slide
diariamente dya·rya·*men·*te daily
dinero ⓜ dee·*ne·*ro money
— en efectivo en e·fek·*tee·*vo cash
dirección ⓕ dee·rek·*thyon* address
disco ⓜ *dees·*ko disk
dólar ⓜ *do·*lar dollar
dolor ⓜ do·*lor* pain
— de cabeza de ka·*be·*tha headache
— de estómago de es·*to·*ma·go stomachache
— de muelas de *mwe·*las toothache
donde *don·*de where
dormir dor·*meer* sleep
dos camas dos *ka·*mas twin beds
ducha ⓕ *doo·*cha shower
dulce *dool·*the sweet
duro/a ⓜ/ⓕ *doo·*ro/a hard

-e-

edificio ⓜ e·dee·*fee·*thyo building
embajada ⓕ em·ba·*kha·*da embassy
embarazada em·ba·ra·*tha·*da pregnant
en en in • on
enfermero/a ⓜ/ⓕ en·fer·*me·*ro/a nurse
enfermo/a ⓜ/ⓕ en·*fer·*mo/a sick
entrar en·*trar* enter
enviar en·vee·*ar* send • ship off
equipaje ⓜ e·kee·*pa·*khe luggage
escalera ⓕ es·ka·*le·*ra stairway
Escocia ⓕ es·*ko·*thya Scotland
escribir es·kree·*beer* write
escuchar es·koo·*char* listen
escuela ⓕ es·*kwe·*la school
espalda ⓕ es·*pal·*da back (body)
espectáculo ⓜ es·pek·*ta·*koo·lo show
esperar es·pe·*rar* wait
esposa ⓕ es·*po·*sa wife
espuma ⓕ **de afeitar** es·*poo·*ma de a·fey·*tar* shaving cream
esquí ⓜ es·*kee* skiing
esta noche es·ta *no·*che tonight
éste/a ⓜ/ⓕ *es·*te/a this
estación ⓕ es·ta·*thyon* season • station
— de autobuses/autocares de ow·to·*boo·*ses/ow·to·*ka·*res (city/intercity) bus station
— de metro de *me·*tro metro station
— de tren de tren railway station
estacionar es·ta·thyo·*nar* park (car)
estómago ⓜ es·*to·*ma·go stomach
estudiante ⓜ&ⓕ es·too·*dyan·*te student
excursión ⓕ eks·koor·*syon* tour
excursionismo ⓜ eks·koor·syo·*nees·*mo hiking
exposición ⓕ eks·po·see·*thyon* exhibition
extranjero/a ⓜ/ⓕ eks·tran·*khe·*ro/a foreign

-f-

facturación ⓕ **de equipajes** fak·too·ra·*thyon* de e·kee·*pa·*khes check-in

falda ① *fal*·da skirt
farmacia ① far·*ma*·thya chemist
(shop) • pharmacy
fecha ① *fe*·cha date (time)
— de nacimiento de na·thee·*myen*·to
date of birth
fiebre ① *fye*·bre fever
fiesta ① *fyes*·ta party
fotografía ① fo·to·gra·*fee*·a
photograph
fotógrafo/a ⓜ/① fo·to·gra·fo/a
photographer
frágil *fra*·kheel fragile
frenos ⓜ pl *fre*·nos brakes
frío/a ⓜ/① *free*·o/a cold
frontera ① fron·*te*·ra border
fruta ① *froo*·ta fruit
fumar foo·*mar* smoke

- g -

gafas ① pl *ga*·fas glasses
— de sol de sol sunglasses
garganta ① gar·*gan*·ta throat
gasolina ① ga·so·*lee*·na petrol
gasolinera ① ga·so·lee·*ne*·ra service
station
gordo/a ⓜ/① *gor*·do/a fat
grande *gran*·de big • large
grandes almacenes ⓜ pl *gran*·des
al·ma·*the*·nes department store
gratis *gra*·tees free (of charge)
grifo ⓜ *gree*·fo tap
gripe ① *gree*·pe influenza
guardarropa ⓜ gwar·da·*ro*·pa
cloakroom
guardería ① gwar·de·*ree*·a
childminding service • creche
guía ⓜ&① *gee*·a guide (person)
guía ① *gee*·a guidebook

- h -

habitación ① a·bee·ta·*thyon*
bedroom • room

— con dos camas kon dos *ka*·mas
twin room
— doble *do*·ble double room
— individual een·dee·vee·*dwal* single
room
hablar a·*blar* speak • talk
helado ⓜ e·*la*·do ice cream
hermana ① er·*ma*·na sister
hermano ⓜ er·*ma*·no brother
hermoso/a ⓜ/① er·*mo*·so/a
beautiful
hielo ⓜ *ye*·lo ice
hija ① *ee*·kha daughter
hijo ⓜ *ee*·kho son
hijos ⓜ pl *ee*·khos children
hombre ⓜ *om*·bre man
hombros ⓜ pl *om*·bros shoulders
hora ① *o*·ra time
horario ⓜ o·*ra*·ryo timetable
hoy oy today

- i -

idiomas ⓜ pl ee·*dyo*·mas languages
iglesia ① ee·*gle*·sya church
impermeable ⓜ eem·per·me·*a*·ble
raincoat
incluido een·kloo·*ee*·do included
Inglaterra ① een·gla·*te*·ra England
inglés ⓜ een·*gles* English
ir eer go
— de compras de *kom*·pras go shopping
— de excursión de eks·koor·*syon* hike
isla ① *ees*·la island

- j -

jabón ⓜ kha·*bon* soap
joyería ① kho·ye·*ree*·a jeweller (shop)
juntos/as ⓜ/① pl *khoon*·tos/as
together

- l -

lago ⓜ *la*·go lake

lana ① *la*·na wool
lápiz ⓜ *la*·peeth pencil
largo/a ⓜ/① *lar*·go/a long
lavadero ⓜ la·va·de·ro laundry
lavandería ① la·van·de·ree·a laundrette
lavar la·*var* wash (something)
leche ① *le*·che milk
lejos *le*·khos far
libra ① *lee*·bra pound (money/weight)
libre *lee*·bre free (not bound)
librería ① lee·bre·*ree*·a bookshop
libro ⓜ *lee*·bro book
limpieza ① leem·*pye*·tha cleaning
llave ① *lya*·ve key
llegadas ① pl lye·*ga*·das arrivals
llegar lye·*gar* arrive
lleno/a ⓜ/① *lye*·no/a full
Los Estados ⓜ pl **Unidos** los es·*ta*·dos oo·*nee*·dos USA
luz ① looth light

- m -

madre ① *ma*·dre mother
maleta ① ma·*le*·ta suitcase
malo/a ⓜ/① *ma*·lo/a bad
mano ① *ma*·no hand
manta ① *man*·ta blanket
mapa ⓜ *ma*·pa map
maquillaje ⓜ ma·kee·*lya*·khe make-up
marido ⓜ ma·*ree*·do husband
matrícula ① ma·*tree*·koo·la license plate number
medio/a ⓜ/① *me*·dyo/a half
mejor me·*khor* better • best
mercado ⓜ mer·*ka*·do market
minusválido/a ⓜ/① mee·noos·*va*·lee·do/a disabled
mochila ① mo·*chee*·la backpack
monedas ① pl mo·*ne*·das coins
montaña ① mon·*ta*·nya mountain
motocicleta ① mo·to·thee·*kle*·ta motorcycle

muebles ⓜ pl *mwe*·bles furniture
mujer ① moo·*kher* wife • woman
multa ① *mool*·ta fine
museo ⓜ moo·*se*·o museum
— de arte de *ar*·te art gallery

- n -

nada *na*·da none • nothing
nadar na·*dar* swim
nariz ① na·*reeth* nose
navaja ① na·*va*·kha penknife
Navidad ① na·vee·*da* Christmas
negocio ⓜ **de artículos básicos** ne·*go*·thyo de ar·*tee*·koo·los *ba*·see·kos convenience store
negocios ⓜ pl ne·*go*·thyos business
neumático ⓜ ne·oo·*ma*·tee·ko tyre
nevera ① ne·*ve*·ra refrigerator
nieto/a ⓜ/① *nye*·to/a grandchild
nieve ① *nye*·ve snow
niño/a ⓜ/① *nee*·nyo/a child
no fumadores no foo·ma·*do*·res non-smoking
noche ① *no*·che evening • night
Nochevieja ① no·che·*vye*·kha New Year's Eve
nombre ⓜ *nom*·bre name
— de pila de *pee*·la first name
norte ⓜ *nor*·te north
noticias ① pl no·*tee*·thyas news
novia ① *no*·vya girlfriend
novio ⓜ *no*·vyo boyfriend
nuestro/a ⓜ/① *nwes*·tro/a our
Nueva Zelanda ① *nwe*·va the·*lan*·da New Zealand
nuevo/a ⓜ/① *nwe*·vo/a new
número ⓜ *noo*·me·ro number

- o -

objetivo ⓜ ob·khe·*tee*·vo lens
obra ① *o*·bra play • building site
ocupado/a ⓜ/① o·koo·*pa*·do/a busy
ocupar o·koo·*par* live (somewhere)

oeste ⓜ o·es·te west
oficina ⓕ o·fee·*thee*·na office
— de objetos perdidos de ob·*khe*·tos per·*dee*·dos lost property office
— de turismo de too·*rees*·mo tourist office
ojo ⓜ o·kho eye
olor ⓜ o·*lor* smell
ordenador ⓜ or·de·na·*dor* computer
— portátil por·ta·teel laptop
oreja ⓕ o·re·kha ear
oscuro/a ⓜ/ⓕ os·koo·ro/a dark
otra vez o·tra veth again
otro/a ⓜ/ⓕ o·tro/a other • another

- p -

padre ⓜ pa·dre father
padres ⓜ pl pa·dres parents
pagar pa·*gar* pay
pago ⓜ pa·go payment
palacio ⓜ pa·*la*·thyo palace
pan ⓜ pan bread
panadería ⓕ pa·na·de·ree·a bakery
pañal ⓜ pa·*nyal* diaper • nappy
pantalones ⓜ pl pan·ta·*lo*·nes pants • trousers
— cortos kor·tos shorts
pañuelos ⓜ pl **de papel** pa·*nywe*·los de pa·*pel* tissues
papel ⓜ pa·*pel* paper
— higiénico ee·*khye*·nee·ko toilet paper
papeles ⓜ pl **del coche** pa·pe·les del ko·che car owner's title
paquete ⓜ pa·ke·te packet • package • wear
parada ⓕ pa·*ra*·da stop
— de autobús de ow·to·*boos* bus stop
— de taxis de ta·ksees taxi stand
paraguas ⓜ pa·*ra*·gwas umbrella
parar pa·*rar* stop
parque ⓜ par·ke park
pasado ⓜ pa·*sa*·do past
pasajero ⓜ pa·sa·*khe*·ro passenger

pasaporte ⓜ pa·sa·*por*·te passport
Pascua ⓕ pas·kwa Easter
pastelería ⓕ pas·te·le·*ree*·a cake shop
pastilla ⓕ pas·*tee*·lya pill
pato ⓜ pa·to duck
pecho ⓜ pe·cho chest
película ⓕ pe·lee·koo·la movie • film (camera)
peligroso/a ⓜ/ⓕ pe·lee·*gro*·so/a dangerous
peluquero/a ⓜ/ⓕ pe·loo·ke·ro/a hairdresser
pensión ⓕ pen·*syon* boarding house
pensionista ⓜ&ⓕ pen·syo·*nees*·ta pensioner
pequeño/a ⓜ/ⓕ pe·ke·nyo/a small
perdido/a ⓜ/ⓕ per·dee·do/a lost
periódico ⓜ pe·*ryo*·dee·ko newspaper
periodista ⓜ&ⓕ pe·ryo·*dees*·ta journalist
pesca ⓕ pes·ka fishing
pescadería ⓕ pes·ka·de·*ree*·a fish shop
pescado ⓜ pes·*ka*·do fish (as food)
pez ⓜ peth fish
pie ⓜ pye foot
pierna ⓕ *pyer*·na leg
pila ⓕ pee·la battery (small)
pintalabios ⓜ peen·ta·*la*·byos lipstick
pintura ⓕ peen·*too*·ra painting
piscina ⓕ pees·*thee*·na swimming pool
plancha ⓕ plan·cha iron
plata ⓕ pla·ta silver
playa ⓕ pla·ya beach
policía ⓕ po·lee·*thee*·a police
pollo ⓜ po·lyo chicken
postal ⓕ pos·*tal* postcard
precio ⓜ pre·thyo price
— de entrada de en·*tra*·da admission price
— del cubierto del koo·*byer*·to cover charge

primavera ① pree·ma·ve·ra spring (season)

primero/a ⑩/① pree·me·ro/a first

privado/a ⑩/① pree·va·do/a private

probar pro·bar try

productos ⑩ pl **alimentarios** pro·dook·tos a·lee·men·ta·ryos foodstuffs

productos ⑩ pl **congelados** pro·dook·tos kon·khe·la·dos frozen foods

profesor(a) ⑩/① pro·fe·sor/ pro·fe·so·ra lecturer • instructor • teacher

prometida ① pro·me·tee·da fiancee

prometido ⑩ pro·me·tee·do fiance

pronto pron·to soon

propina ① pro·pee·na tip

pub ⑩ poob bar (with music) • pub

pueblo ⑩ pwe·blo village

puente ⑩ pwen·te bridge

puesta ① **del sol** pwes·ta del sol sunset

~ *q* ~

quemadura ① ke·ma·doo·ra burn

— de sol de sol sunburn

queso ⑩ ke·so cheese

quien kyen who

quincena ① keen·the·na fortnight

quiosco ⑩ kyos·ko news stand • newsagency

~ *r* ~

rápido/a ⑩/① ra·pee·do/a fast

raro/a ⑩/① ra·ro/a rare (item)

recibo ⑩ re·thee·bo receipt

recorrido ⑩ **guiado** re·ko·ree·do gee·a·do guided tour

recuerdo ⑩ re·kwer·do souvenir

reembolsar re·em·bol·sar refund

regalo ⑩ re·ga·lo gift

reloj ⑩ **de pulsera** re·lokh de pool·se·ra watch

reserva ① re·ser·va reservation

reservar re·ser·var book/reserve

resfriado ⑩ res·free·a·do cold

rodilla ① ro·dee·lya knee

ropa ① ro·pa clothing

— de cama de ka·ma bedding

— interior een·te·ryor underwear

roto/a ⑩/① ro·to/a broken

ruidoso/a ⑩/① rwee·do·so/a loud

ruinas ① pl rwee·nas ruins

~ *s* ~

sábana ① sa·ba·na sheet (bed)

sabroso/a ⑩/① sa·bro·so/a tasty

saco ⑩ **de dormir** sa·ko de dor·meer sleeping bag

sala ① **de espera** sa·la de es·pe·ra waiting room

sala ① **de tránsito** sa·la de tran·see·to transit lounge

salida ① sa·lee·da departure • exit

salir con sa·leer kon go out with

salir de sa·leer de depart

salón de belleza ⑩ sa·lon de be·lye·tha beauty salon

sangre ① san·gre blood

sastre ⑩ sas·tre tailor

seda ① se·da silk

segundo/a ⑩/① se·goon·do/a second

seguro ⑩ se·goo·ro insurance

sello ⑩ se·lyo stamp

semáforos ⑩ pl se·ma·fo·ros traffic lights

sendero ⑩ sen·de·ro mountain path • path

servicio ⑩ ser·vee·thyo service charge

servicios ⑩ pl ser·vee·thyos toilets

sexo ⑩ se·kso sex

— seguro se·goo·ro safe sex

silla ① see·lya chair

— de ruedas de rwe·das wheelchair

sin seen without

sobre ⑩ so·bre envelope

sol ⓜ *sol* sun
solo/a ⓜ/ⓕ *so*·lo/a alone
soltero/a ⓜ/ⓕ sol·*te*·ro/a single
sombrero ⓜ som·*bre*·ro hat
subtítulos ⓜ pl soob·*tee*·too·los subtitles
sucio/a ⓜ/ⓕ *soo*·thyo/a dirty
sujetador ⓜ soo·khe·ta·*dor* bra
supermercado ⓜ soo·per·mer·*ka*·do supermarket
sur ⓜ *soor* south

- t -

talla ⓕ *ta*·lya size (clothes)
taquilla ⓕ ta·*kee*·lya ticket office
tarde *tar*·de late
tarjeta tar·*khe*·ta card
— de crédito de *kre*·dee·to credit card
— de embarque de em·*bar*·ke boarding pass
tasa ⓕ **del aeropuerto** *ta*·sa del ay·ro·*pwer*·to airport tax
teatro ⓜ te·*a*·tro theatre
tele ⓕ *te*·le TV
teléfono ⓜ te·*le*·fo·no telephone
— móvil *mo*·veel mobile phone
templado/a ⓜ/ⓕ tem·*pla*·do/a warm
temprano tem·*pra*·no early
tenedor ⓜ te·ne·*dor* fork
tentempié ⓜ ten·tem·*pye* snack
tía ⓕ *tee*·a aunt
tienda ⓕ *tyen*·da shop
— de comestibles de ko·mes·*tee*·bles grocery
— de recuerdos de re·*kwer*·dos souvenirs
— de ropa de *ro*·pa clothing
— deportiva de·por·*tee*·va sports
tijeras ⓕ pl tee·*khe*·ras scissors
tipo ⓜ **de cambio** *tee*·po de *kam*·byo exchange rate
tirar tee·*rar* pull
toalla ⓕ to·*a*·lya towel
tobillo ⓜ to·*bee*·lyo ankle
todo *to*·do all • everything

torcedura ⓕ tor·the·*doo*·ra sprain
toro ⓜ *to*·ro bull
torre ⓕ *to*·re tower
tos ⓕ *tos* cough
tostada ⓕ tos·*ta*·da toast
tostadora ⓕ tos·ta·*do*·ra toaster
trabajo ⓜ tra·*ba*·kho job • work
traducir tra·doo·*theer* translate
tranquilo/a ⓜ/ⓕ tran·*kee*·lo/a quiet
tranvía ⓕ tran·*vee*·a tram
tren ⓜ *tren* train
turista ⓜ&ⓕ too·*rees*·ta tourist

- u -

universidad ⓕ oo·nee·ver·see·*da* university
urgente oor·*khen*·te urgent

- v -

vacaciones ⓕ pl va·ka·*thyo*·nes holidays • vacation
vacío/a ⓜ/ⓕ va·*thee*·o/a empty
vacuna ⓕ va·*koo*·na vaccination
validar va·lee·*dar* validate
vaqueros ⓜ pl va·*ke*·ros jeans
vaso ⓜ *va*·so (drinking) glass
venir ve·*neer* come
ventana ⓕ ven·*ta*·na window
ventilador ⓜ ven·tee·la·*dor* fan
verano ⓜ ve·*ra*·no summer
verduras ⓕ pl ver·*doo*·ras vegetables
vestido ⓜ ves·*tee*·do dress
vestuarios ⓜ pl ves·*twa*·ryos changing room
viejo/a ⓜ/ⓕ *vye*·kho/a old
vino ⓜ *vee*·no wine
volver vol·*ver* return

- z -

zapatería ⓕ tha·pa·te·*ree*·a shoe shop
zapatos ⓜ pl tha·*pa*·tos shoes

Index

91

INDEX

INDEX

Acknowledgments

Associate Product Director Angela Tinson
Product Editor Shona Gray
Language Writers Marta López, Cristina Hernández Montero
Cover Designer Campbell McKenzie

Thanks

Kate Chapman, Gwen Cotter, James Hardy, Indra Kilfoyle,
Wibowo Rusli, Juan Winata

Published by Lonely Planet Global Ltd
CRN 554153

4th Edition – June 2018
Text © Lonely Planet 2018
Cover Image Donostia-San Sebastián – Guido Cozzi/4Corners ©

Printed in China   10 9 8 7 6 5 4 3 2

Contact lonelyplanet.com/contact

10. Phrases to Get You Talking

Hello.	Hola. *o·la*
Goodbye.	Adiós. *a·dyos*
Please.	Por favor. *por fa·vor*
Thank you.	Gracias. *gra·thyas*
Excuse me.	Perdón. *per·don*
Sorry.	Lo siento. *lo syen·to*
Yes.	Sí. *see*
No.	No. *no*
I don't understand.	No entiendo. *no en·tyen·do*
How much is it?	¿Cuánto cuesta? *kwan·to kwes·ta*